Bride's Book
of Etiquette

Bride's Book of Etiquette

by the Editors of Bride's

Third Edition
Revised and Updated

GROSSET & DUNLAP
Publishers
New York

Published simultaneously in Canada
Library of Congress Catalog Card Number: 72–90862
ISBN: 0–448–01562–5

Fifth Printing

Printed in the United States of America

FOREWORD

CONGRATULATIONS! YOU'RE GETTING married, and we're delighted. If the one check on your happiness is confusion over wedding plans, relax. This book was planned to help you make every one of the choices that follow the delicious decision to get married.

Your *Bride's Book of Etiquette* is simply the written-down version of the way things are done. We're concerned not about who is right, but about what will make everyone involved in an important event happy, comfortable and thoroughly able to enjoy this great celebration in your life.

In this new edition, we've tried to anticipate every situation you might encounter. Not every couple has just four parents who live in the same town where the couple grew up, will marry and finally settle down. And more and more couples are taking one step ahead of tradition to suit their weddings to the times. We want to help.

Naturally we cannot anticipate every question, so if you can't follow the rules without flying in the face of family or community tradition or your own dearest wishes, by all means bend the rule.

That's what it's all about, after all: to have your wedding day the happiest imaginable for your families, for the larger community you are joining and most especially for you, the bride and groom to whom we dedicate this book.

ANN CYNTHIA DIAMOND
Copy and Features Editor
Bride's

CONTENTS

Bride's Book
of Etiquette

1
Your Engagement

ONCE YOU'VE DECIDED to get married, chances are you'll want to announce your engagement. Even if you don't wear a ring, there is a moment of decision after which, for example, your mother may tell her manicurist, yes, in fact, Julie is getting married, probably in July.

There are time-honored methods for announcing an engagement, as there are for most of the pleasant duties surrounding a marriage. And most of them are fun.

YOUR FAMILY FIRST

Your family deserves to hear the good news first from you, not from the mother of a girlfriend you just couldn't wait to tell. Even if you live away from home, long-distance telephone or jet travel can make this your first act as an engaged couple.

How you tell your parents is up to you. If they've known your fiancé forever and he is often at the house, you might share your news at dinner. If your parents do not know your fiancé well, or you can't be sure how they'll react to your decision, or you just can't wait for a day to tell them together, then tell them yourself. (Remember Luci Johnson crawling in bed with her parents to share the news.)

In either case, your fiancé should speak privately to your father as soon as possible. Not so much to ask for your hand — although many fathers appreciate this old-fashioned courtesy — but to receive congratulations, welcome and, usually, advice as well.

If your father isn't living, your mother, stepfather, guardian or whoever lives with you may receive your fiancé. If your parents are divorced, he will see both parents in turn.

If you live far away from your parents and telephone to tell them the news, your fiancé should write to your father, expressing his good intentions. And he should visit your parents, if possible, as soon as he can.

Naturally, you'll want to tell his parents right away, too. Tradition requires that they "call on" your family as soon as possible. Today his mother might drop your mother a note, or she might telephone to invite your parents for drinks, dinner or Sunday brunch. In short, any way his parents usually entertain their friends is a good way for them to get to know your parents. Even if they're old friends, this is a good time for them to have dinner together and celebrate. You two — and your brothers and sisters — may or may not be included in this gathering, but it should not be a big party. Time enough for that after the engagement is announced.

By the way, this is the sort of occasion on which a future mother-in-law blurts, "Oh, call me Marjorie!" (or Mom or Mother B.). Or she may ask what you want to call her, and you might suggest whatever her own children call her, unless that's what you call your own mother. Or you might use her first name. Until she brings it up, however, go right on calling her Mrs. Jones.

If your groom's parents do not make the first move, your own mother might telephone and invite them. Better to reverse etiquette than to risk hard feelings.

If your parents are divorced, this courtesy call is usually first extended from and to the parents with whom you live. If your parents live in different towns, your fiancé's mother writes to your mother to say how pleased she is to welcome you into the family. In this case, your fiancé's mother may also invite you to spend a few days with them.

LENGTH OF ENGAGEMENT

You are engaged as soon as you decide to get married and receive your parents' blessing. But you need not announce your engagement publicly until you begin making plans for the wedding. If you are going to wait a long time — until your fiancé completes his military service or until after graduation, for example — you should postpone your official announcement until a year or less before the wedding. This gives you plenty of time to plan the most elaborate formal wedding — and a bang-up honeymoon.

PUBLISHING THE NEWS

Once you've told your parents, close relatives and best friends in person, by telephone or by personal notes, your engagement may be announced in the newspapers of your home towns. Since policies vary from paper to paper, it's best to check with the society editor in advance about the proper form, deadlines, photographs, etc. Some papers, for example, accept information over the telephone, while others insist that you complete a special printed form at least ten days before publication. Some papers publish exclusive photographs only, while others publish either engagement or wedding pictures, but not both. If your newspaper does not supply printed forms, submit the necessary information to the society editor. Type it, double spaced, on one side of a sheet of paper 8½ × 11 inches. In the upper right-hand corner, put the name, address and telephone number of your parents or someone in the community who can be called for verification. Be sure to mention the date on which you want the announcement to appear.

The simplest and preferred form:

Mr. and Mrs. John Brown of Dayton Avenue announce the engagement of their daughter, Helen Louise, to Mr. Stanley Forsythe, the son of Mr. and Mrs. Hugh S. Forsythe of Pasadena. No date has been set for the wedding. (Or, The wedding will take place in April.)

A longer form might read:

Mr. and Mrs. John Brown of Dayton Avenue announce the engagement of their daughter, Helen Louise to Mr. Stanley

Forsythe, the son of Mr. and Mrs. Hugh S. Forsythe of Pasadena. Miss Brown was graduated from Miss Spencer's School and from Seaton College in 19xx. She is the granddaughter of Mr. and Mrs. Alexander Brown of this city and of Mrs. Norman Hoyt and the late Justice Hoyt of Hamilton, Ohio. Mr. Forsythe attended Pilcher Academy and graduated from State University in the class of 19xx. He is now associated with the United Cement Corporation. The wedding will take place April 10, at Trinity Methodist Church.

If one of your parents has died, your announcement might read:

The engagement of Miss Helen Louise Brown, daughter of Mrs. John Brown and the late Mr. Brown, to Mr. Stanley Forsythe, the son of Mr. and Mrs. Hugh S. Forsythe of Pasadena, is announced by the bride's mother.

If your parents are divorced, the announcement is made by the parent with whom you live, but both parents are mentioned in the story:

Mrs. Hoyt Brown (a combination of her maiden and married surnames) *announces the engagement of her daughter, Helen Louise, to Mr. Stanley Forsythe, the son of Mr. and Mrs. Hugh S. Forsythe of Pasadena. Miss Brown is the daughter also of Mr. John Brown of San Francisco.*

Some newspapers also include information about military service, club memberships or college associations, but there is no need to mention such facts unless they are customarily published in your paper. When in doubt, be brief and to the point. The editor can always call you if she wants more details. If you send a photograph with your announcement, it should be an 8 × 10 inch glossy portrait (5 × 7 inch is also acceptable). Be sure to attach a typed line of identification to the photograph and to protect it with a piece of stiff cardboard.

AN ANNOUNCEMENT PARTY

Naturally, anyone may give a party in your honor, but your parents are likely to be among the most eager to do so. If your parents do have a party, it should be the first one celebrating your engagement. It may be held before or shortly after the public announcement. This might be a tea, a dinner or a cocktail party. "In honor of Howard and Carol" might be written on the invitations. You two might stand in an informal receiving line with your parents and your fiancé's. Or you might simply count on the guests' intuition, your ring and your own happy smile to convey the good news. In any case, sometime during the evening your father should propose a toast to the two of you. Your fiancé traditionally responds by drinking to you and your parents. Do you feel like the center of attention? Right again.

Your fiancé's mother may want to give a party to introduce you to her family and friends. This might be a luncheon, a tea or a family dinner, but it should not be a shower.

Be sure to thank in writing anyone who entertains for you, even with as simple an outing as a family lunch at Grandmother's. It earns you a reputation for thoughtfulness that will stand you in good stead throughout your married life.

ENGAGEMENT PRESENTS

Your first engagement present will probably be your ring, although a ring is by no means necessary to being engaged. In fact, many girls prefer a really handsome wedding ring when economy narrows the field. A single diamond for fidelity and purity is the traditional choice, but other precious or semiprecious stones are beautiful and often easier on the budget. Or you may choose an unusual setting incorporating smaller diamonds. An engagement ring doesn't have to be new. A man can pay no greater compliment to his future bride than to give her an heirloom ring or to have family stones reset in the style she chooses.

You do not have to give your fiancé an engagement present, but many girls choose to do so. It's usually something personal and lasting. For example, you might give him a handsomely bound edition of his favorite book or a wristwatch. In addition to your ring — or in place of it — your fiancé may wish to give you another gift. He may choose anything except clothing, a house or a car, the things that indicate material support.

An engagement is not usually a gift-giving occasion, but close family friends and relatives often give heirlooms or trousseau things. Whatever you are given, be as prompt in thanking the givers as you can. A written note is the most gracious and thoughtful way to show your appreciation, even if you have expressed your thanks in person when you received the gift.

ENGAGEMENT PROPRIETY

Now that you're engaged, your behavior is under a new kind of scrutiny. You may think it's none of Aunt Harriet's business if you two drive cross-country together, but Aunt Harriet can make it her business to make you unwelcome in your new family. Being discreet beats starting arguments with tactless truth.

Naturally, you will continue to see your other friends of both sexes. But you shouldn't do anything — like staying up all night talking with an old beau — that will cause the community to doubt the sincerity of your decision to pledge yourself to one man.

Excessive public displays of affection are no more appropriate now than they were before you became engaged.

BROKEN ENGAGEMENTS

If you decide to call it off, count yourself lucky to have avoided the agony of divorce. Send a release to every paper that announced your engagement, reading:

The engagement of Miss Ann Smith and Mr. Jacob Jones has been terminated by mutual consent.

Return any presents that were given as engagement gifts, including your ring. While you need not return gifts that were given you for birthdays or holidays, his family will appreciate the return of any family heirlooms.

If it's a last-minute decision, wedding invitations will have to be recalled by notes, calls and telegrams (see Chapter V), and all wedding presents sent back to the donors. Just as for an engagement, you should try to write brief notes to close friends and family telling them of your decision. There is no need to offer an explanation. The less said, the less fuss made, the sooner the whole thing will be forgotten.

In the tragic case of a fiancé's death before the wedding, the presents must also be returned by some member of the family.

2
Pre-Wedding Parties

AN ENGAGEMENT IS one of the best occasions for party-giving, and your friends and family will surely rise to it. You may be honored at anything from a breakfast to a midnight supper, over tea or cocktails, indoors or out. There are no rules governing engagement parties, so your friends may demonstrate their hospitality in any way they like. Your only duties are to show your pleasure, act surprised when you're supposed to and follow each event with a note of thanks to the hosts. Take care, too, that your parties are well-timed so you don't become overtired and sleepwalk through your wedding.

SHOWERS

According to folklore, the first shower was given to replace the dowry denied a bride who married against her father's wishes. Modern showers, too, help a couple equip their new home. Even if you have two of all the basics from your own apartments, there are always extras that you'd welcome, but might not buy.

Almost any party at any hour of the day is suitable for a shower. It might be a morning coffee or brunch, an afternoon tea or luncheon, or an evening dinner or coffee and dessert. In short, it can be anything that is convenient for you and your hostess. The food and decorations may be as simple or as elaborate as the hostess cares to make them. The gifts they bring — and your enjoyment of them — are usually all the entertainment the guests expect. Invitations may be issued over the telephone, on printed cards or in any manner devised by the hostess. For example, invitations to a kitchen shower might be printed on the back of grocery receipts, while those for a game shower might be attached to playing cards.

Only the hostess and the guest list for a shower fall under the rules of etiquette. The most likely hostess is your maid of honor or a bridesmaid, but good friends, cousins and aunts often take part. In fact, anyone may give a shower in your honor except your mother or stepmother, your sisters or members of your fiancé's immediate family. (They are so close to you it's almost like requesting gifts for yourself.)

The guest list usually includes the maid of honor and bridesmaids and the mothers, sisters, and other close relatives of both the bride and groom. Showers given by co-workers, club members or school friends, however, usually include only members of that group. Since every shower guest is expected to bring a gift, only close friends and relatives are invited. And because too many bridesmaids giving showers is a bit harsh on your friends' budgets, you might suggest that they get together on a single shower. The groom attends the showers if they are mixed parties to which the husbands and boyfriends of other guests are also invited. These mixed parties are appropriate — and more fun — for any shower but a personal shower for the bride.

Shower gifts are relatively small and inexpensive supplements to wedding presents. Almost anything the couple can use is appropriate, but the hostess usually designates a specific gift category (such as linen or lingerie). Since many showers are planned as surprise parties, you'd be wise to make your preferences known to your mother, your maid of honor and anyone else who might be consulted.

SHOWER THEMES

Kitchen showers are the most popular, because of the enormous range of inexpensive gadgets every couple needs. Novice cooks — especially those who have never had apartments of their own — need everything from pots and pans, small appliances and utensils to wastebaskets, mops and brooms and sponges.

If the guest list is rich in experienced cooks, the hostess might suggest that each bring a recipe and one needed item (a flour sifter with a cake recipe, a mold with a soufflé recipe, a salad bowl with a dressing recipe.) If uniform recipe cards are sent out with the invitations, the hostess can assemble them in a recipe box or notebook for the bride.

If a couple of adventurous eaters are setting up home

nearby, a supply of fancy canned goods might be welcome.

If you'll be leaving town after the wedding, tea towels and aprons, pastry tubes, salad baskets, trivets, trays, knives and small gadgets travel well. Or a subscription to a fruit- or food-of-the-month club or a gourmet magazine might be sent to your new home.

A personal clothing shower could include all the frilly night things or underwear that have long been the staple of all-girl showers. Other gifts: closet accessories like shoebags, hangers, scarf or glove boxes, a sewing box with all the necessary accessories — tiny scissors, spare buttons and pins.

If you've chosen your color scheme, a linen and bath shower can gift you with table linens, sheets, pillow cases and blankets, towels and bath accessories: a scale, tissue box, soaps, wastebasket, even an electric shoe polisher.

An entertainment shower might gift you and your groom with bar things from a special bottle of Scotch to a corkscrew and coasters; games from Monopoly to a miniature roulette wheel; cards, chips or chessboard; books and records guests know you'll enjoy or tickets to the theatre or ballet for after you return from your honeymoon.

Besides these popular shower ideas, the lifestyle of the bride and groom may suggest more specialized themes: the garden shower if you have a backyard or green thumb; a travel shower — with gifts of insect repellent and phrase books — if you will be going overseas.

The party's hour should suit the theme: a barbecue or cocktail party for a mixed entertainment shower; a champagne breakfast or tea for a personal shower.

Naturally your exuberant verbal thanks contribute to the fun of the party itself, but you really should follow up with a note, particularly to those friends you don't see every day. (Of course anyone who sent gifts but did not come must be thanked in writing.) If your groom attended the shower, he could take on the notes to those special friends of his whom you don't know.

BRIDESMAIDS' PARTIES

It is customary for the bridesmaids — collectively or individually — to entertain for the bride, but they are not required to do so. If some of them come from far away, it's usually a joint party, perhaps a luncheon, at a club or hotel. Local girls are more likely to entertain at home. If they wish, your bridesmaids may give you their wedding presents at this party.

Or you may give a party for your bridesmaids. This may be a luncheon, a tea or a small dinner held the same night as the bachelor dinner. It may serve to introduce out-of-town bridesmaids to your other friends, to show your wedding gifts to your attendants or to give your bridesmaids a chance to try on their dresses. It's also an ideal time for you to give your presents to your attendants. Whatever form the party takes, you may want to serve the traditional pink bride's cake in which a symbolic ring, coin or thimble is baked. According to legend, the girl whose slice of cake contains the trinket will be the next bride.

BACHELOR PARTY

The bachelor dinner is an optional custom popular in many areas. It was originally planned as the groom's last fling with the boys the night before his wedding. Today's bachelor dinner serves the same purpose as the bridesmaids' party. Your groom may give a bachelor party for his attendants or the groom's friends may pool their resources to give a dinner for him. In either event, the groom usually takes advantage of the occasion to present gifts to his best man and ushers.

At some time during the party, he also proposes a traditional toast to his bride. After everyone has drunk the toast — usually champagne — it's customary to break the glasses so they may never be used for a less worthy purpose. If your fiancé plans to follow this tradition, he should arrange to use inexpensive glasses. As more drinking usually follows this first sentimental libation, it's wise to schedule the dinner two or three nights before the wedding to ensure a sober wedding party.

REHEARSAL DINNER

A rehearsal dinner for members of the wedding party is customary. Your fiancé's parents, your own family or close friends may sponsor the party. It may be held at home, in a club or restaurant or at a hotel. If your wedding party is not too large, a few good friends or relatives, particularly those from out of town, may be invited. Decorations should be kept simple. A toast to the bride and groom is usually proposed during the dinner, often by the best man. The groom may respond by toasting his bride and her parents.

If you haven't already done so, you and your fiancé may want to take this opportunity to distribute gifts to your attendants. The rehearsal is usually scheduled to precede the dinner. If the rehearsal follows, be sure that everyone will be able to get to the rehearsal on time and sober.

WEDDING DAY BREAKFAST

Sometimes a friend will offer to invite the out-of-town wedding guests for a brunch before an afternoon wedding. The bride and groom are not expected to show up at such a gathering, as its purpose is to free them and their immediate families for last minute preparations.

3
Wedding Customs

Most WEDDING CUSTOMS evolved from a wish to symbolize all the good things the union meant to the couple and the community: fertility, constancy, happiness. New customs are being initiated every day to match our changing ideas of what we wish for the new family formed by a marriage. Those that continue to symbolize the same good intentions — a wish for peace or the affirmation of the bride and groom's individual integrity — will flourish. Those that are frivolous or faddish will die of embarrassment. Other, older traditions are gradually outgrown and eventually abandoned, as have been the word "obey" in the wedding vows and certain sacrificial aspects of marriage.

Naturally you'll select your dress, a veil and flowers for their beauty as well as for their traditional significance. But do look over some of these time-honored customs, and choose those that appeal to you and your families' sentiment.

19

THE WHYS AND WHEREFORES

WHY AN ENGAGEMENT RING? The betrothal or pledge ring was first given in the days of marriage by purchase — both as part payment and as a symbol of the prospective groom's good intentions. The earliest pledge rings were made of braided grass, while later ones were fashioned of leather, carved stone and crude metals. The diamond was first incorporated into engagement rings in medieval Italy. This most imperishable of all stones was chosen as a symbol of enduring love.

WHY A WEDDING RING? The circular shape of a ring has symbolized unending love since the days of the early Egyptians. Primitive brides wore rings of rushes or hemp, which had to be replaced every year. Early Romans wore more durable iron rings to symbolize the permanence of marriage, but affluent cultures have long favored the lasting beauty and purity of gold for their wedding bands.

WHY THE THIRD FINGER, LEFT HAND? Ancient peoples believed that the vein in the third finger of the left hand ran directly to the heart. Medieval bridegrooms placed the ring on three of the bride's fingers in turn to symbolize the trinity, "In the name of the Father, Son and Holy Ghost." By "Amen," the band was on the ring finger, where it remained. The English Prayer Book of 1549 specified the left hand for the rings of both bride and groom. Since then it has become the custom for English-speaking people to wear the wedding band and engagement ring on the third finger. In many European countries, however, the wedding ring is worn on the right hand, and Greek women wear their rings on their left hands until they are married, and then move them to the right hand.

WHY THE BRIDAL SHOWER? It is believed that the first bridal shower took place in Holland when a maiden fell in love with a poor miller. Her father forbade their marriage, but the miller's friends "showered" the bride with gifts so she would be able to marry even though she lacked the traditional dowry that would have helped her set up housekeeping.

WHY DOES THE BRIDE WEAR A VEIL? Veils began as a sign of youth and virginity. Greek and Roman brides wore flame-colored veils. Early Christian brides wore white or purple. Anglo-Saxon brides hid their blushes behind their own flowing hair. Even today, in some countries the groom meets his bride veiled and never sees her face until she is legally his. It is said that Nelly Custis began the fashion for bridal veils in this country when she chose to wear a long scarf to her wedding to President Washington's aide, Major Lawrence Lewis. Her decision stemmed from the flattering comments her fiancé made after glimpsing her through a lace curtain at an open window.

WHY DOES THE BRIDE WEAR WHITE? White has been a symbol of purity — in heart's devotion as well as body — and celebration since Roman times.

WHY DOES THE BRIDE CARRY FLOWERS? Ancient

Roman brides carried bunches of herbs under their wedding veils as symbols of fertility and fidelity. Because the orange tree blooms and bears fruit at the same time, the Saracens chose orange blossoms to represent fertility and happiness. Lilies have long symbolized purity, and roses have stood for love. Ivy, used at early Greek weddings as a sign of indissoluble love, is still used to trim wedding bouquets. You might follow a Victorian custom and choose a bouquet to spell out your husband's name: *r*oses, *o*rchids and *b*abies' breath might begin a bouquet for *Rob*ert.

WHY SOMETHING BLUE? The brides of Israel in ancient times wore a blue ribbon on the border of their fringed robes to denote purity, fidelity and love. Blue is also associated with the purity of the Virgin Mary. Today, color psychologists choose blue for calmness and serenity.

WHAT IS THE TROUSSEAU? The word trousseau has its derivation in the French word, *trousse*, which means bundle. Originally a bride took a bundle of clothes and personal possessions with her to her new home. This was later expanded into a more generous dowry that enhanced the value of an unmarried daughter in the eyes of prospective suitors.

WHY IS THE BRIDE GIVEN AWAY? The bride is given away because in early times she was looked on almost as chattel. Her parents arranged her marriage, and she was literally given to the groom. Today, in Protestant ceremonies, to signify his approval of the marriage, the father walks to the altar with his daughter and gives her in marriage. Some fathers respond to the question, "Who gives this woman . . . ?'', ''Her mother and I . . .'' to indicate that they give up, willingly, the first spot in her affection and loyalties.

WHY A WEDDING CAKE? Cake has been a part of wedding celebrations since the ancient Romans broke a thin loaf over the bride's head at the end of the ceremony. The wheat from which it was made was a symbol of fertility, and the crumbs were eagerly sought by the guests as good luck tokens. In England during the Middle Ages it was traditional for the bride and groom to kiss over a pile of small cakes. When an enterprising baker decided to mass all these cakes together and cover them with frosting, the modern, tiered wedding cake was born.

You may have traditional trinkets baked into your cake. A code in the icing tells where they are, so they can be served to the wedding party: a wishbone for luck, a heart for romance, a ring for the next to marry, a gold or silver coin for good fortune.

WHY RICE AND OLD SHOES? In the Orient, rice means ''May you always have a full pantry,'' and a red slipper thrown on the roof of a house indicates that a honeymoon is in progress. Also, among early Hebrews, sandals were often given as evidence of good faith in an exchange of property. Today, casting a shoe after the bride signifies her father's transfer of her devotion to her new husband, while the rice is a token of fertility and a life of plenty.

WHY A HONEYMOON? In ancient marriages by capture, the groom kept his bride in hiding to prevent searching relatives from finding her. The term had its origin when early Teuton couples drank a honey drink, known as mead or metheglin, for thirty days after their wedding or until the moon had waned.

WHY IS THE BRIDE LIFTED OVER THE THRESHHOLD? The Roman bride, demonstrating reluctance to leave her father's house, had to be carried over the threshhold of her new home. It was also believed that evil spirits hovered at the threshhold of the house, so the bride was lifted over to ensure her protection from them.

Apart from the customs that most Americans expect, you might want to borrow one of these special international customs if it has some special meaning or appeal for you.

FOLLOW AN ENGLISH CUSTOM: Have the bells peal as you enter the church to be married, then have them ring another change as you leave on the arm of your new husband.

FOLLOW A SOUTH AMERICAN CUSTOM: Wear a pale blue petticoat under your wedding gown to peep out as something blue.

FOLLOW A EUROPEAN CUSTOM: Have a country wedding and ride to and from the church in a horse-drawn carriage, with the carriage and horses decorated with white flowers and ribbons.

FOLLOW A BERMUDA TRADITION: After the ceremony, help your husband plant a small tree to grow with your marriage.

FOLLOW A FRENCH CUSTOM: Have a *coupe de marriage* at your reception. This small silver bowl or cup with handles at either side is given a place of honor near the wedding cake. At a signal from the best man, you and your groom drink from it in turn. The cup may be engraved with your names or initials and wedding date, then passed on to future generations.

FOLLOW A COLONIAL TRADITION: Wear a beautifully embroidered silk or lace apron tied over your wedding dress to be handed down to future generations.

FOLLOW A BELGIAN CUSTOM: Carry a fine wedding handkerchief. After the wedding, it's embroidered with your name, framed and given a place of honor in your home until the next family bride carries out the same custom, embroidering her name under yours.

FOLLOW AN ANCIENT JEWISH CUSTOM: Marry outdoors and have children as numerous as the stars.

FOLLOW THE ANCIENT WEDDING RHYME: Wear something old, something new, something borrowed, something blue and a lucky sixpence in your shoe.

4
Planning Your Wedding

WHERE AND WHEN

ONE OF THE first things you must decide is when your marriage will take place. Except for the most simple ceremony, you'll need at least two to three months to make all the necessary arrangements. Formal weddings usually need at least six months' planning. When you set the precise date and time of the ceremony, you'll have to consider religious regulations and local custom. Some religions, for example, do not allow formal weddings on certain days of the calendar. Others perform ceremonies only during certain hours. Caterers, too, are often overbooked, so you must be sure your reception site is free on the date you choose. June is a very romantic month for weddings, but romance may wear thin if there is a whole series of weddings at successive hours in a single church or hotel.

A wedding may take place almost anywhere — in a small garden or a large cathedral, in a judge's chambers or a hotel ballroom. Your religious beliefs and the number of guests you expect to have are the primary considerations in choosing a site. A civil ceremony at City Hall meets all the legal requirements, of course, but you may be limited in the number of guests who may share the celebration. A home or chapel setting is suitable for a small wedding, while a Catholic church is required for the celebration of the Nuptial Mass. A Jewish wedding may be performed in a synagogue, but in some areas large ceremonies are held in clubs or hotels.

You and your fiancé need not be active members of a congregation in order to have a religious wedding. Some churches rent all or part of their facilities for a small fee. Special circumstances must be taken into consideration, however, as some churches do not marry persons of different faiths or divorced persons.

It's customary for a wedding to take place in the bride's home town, but this isn't always practical. If you and your fiancé live in a city removed from both sets of parents, for example, it may make more sense to be married there among your mutual friends. As the bride, you have the prerogative to choose the site of the ceremony, but naturally you will consider the wishes of both your parents and your groom in making your decision.

WHAT TYPE OF WEDDING

There are only four basic types of weddings, whether large or small: very formal, formal, semiformal and informal.

Garden weddings, military weddings and double weddings may be variations of any of these.

A VERY FORMAL WEDDING usually includes

A stately dress with a long train and a veil in a complementary length for the bride.

Formal attire (white tie and tails in the evening, cutaways in the daytime) for the groom and all the men in the wedding party.

Four to twelve bridesmaids in floor-length dresses.

Long dresses for the mothers of the bride and groom.

A high noon, late afternoon or evening ceremony.

200 or more guests.

Engraved invitations, usually the large size, with separate reception invitations enclosed.

A large and lavish reception.

A FORMAL WEDDING usually has these characteristics:

A long dress with a chapel or sweep train and a veil for the bride.

Formal clothes (black tie in the evening, stroller jackets with striped trousers in the daytime) for the groom and his attendants.

Two to six bridesmaids, usually in long dresses.

Long or elaborate street-length dresses for the mothers.

Ceremony at any hour of the day.

At least 100 guests.

Engraved invitations, usually with separate reception invitations enclosed.

A festive reception.

A SEMIFORMAL WEDDING usually means

An elaborate street-length dress (or a simple floor-length dress) and a hat or short veil for the bride.

Dark suits for the groom and his attendants.

One or two bridal attendants in street-length dresses.

Street-length dresses for the mothers.

A morning or early afternoon ceremony.

Fewer than 100 guests.

A single engraved invitation to both ceremony and reception.

A small but charming reception.

AN INFORMAL WEDDING is usually characterized by

Street clothes, often a suit, for the bride.

Suits for the groom and best man.

A maid of honor, but no bridesmaids, in street clothes.

A daytime ceremony anywhere, including City Hall.

A guest list including relatives and close friends.

Handwritten or personal invitations to the small ceremony and reception.

In general, the formality of a wedding increases with the size of the guest list. But a wedding before fifty guests in a magnificient church might enjoy all the pomp of formal dress. Or you might invite several hundred guests to a vast and informal ceremony out of doors.

WHAT TYPE OF RECEPTION

A wedding is a solemn ceremony and the reception that follows should be joyous. It's traditional to gather friends and relatives to celebrate the happy day. Some couples have a large reception following an intimate family ceremony. Others invite everyone to the wedding but ask only close friends and relatives to the reception. Or, ideally, of course, you may invite all your guests to both.

The reception should immediately follow the ceremony. After a morning wedding, for example, a light breakfast or luncheon is lovely. If you choose an afternoon wedding, you may serve punch and cake or cocktails and hors d'oeuvres. Late afternoon and evening weddings are often followed by a cocktail reception or a dinner with dancing.

A reception may be held almost anywhere — in a church hall, in your home or garden, at a private club, hotel or restaurant. Adequate kitchen facilities and sufficient space to accomodate your guests are the only requirements. If the reception is considerably smaller than the wedding, you may want to form a receiving line immediately after the ceremony so every guest will have the opportunity to wish you well.

VISITING YOUR CLERGYMAN

When the bride and groom are not of the same faith, the bride usually chooses where to be married. If your fiancé's religious convictions outweigh yours, however, he should choose. Whatever you decide, you and your fiancé should make an appointment to visit the clergyman as soon as possible. This is not only the practical thing to do, it's also a requirement in many religions.

Unless you are both members of the same church, you may have to show certificates of baptism or confirmation to the clergyman in charge before he agrees to perform the ceremony. He may also ask you to present a letter attesting to your marital or religious status. If you're planning a mixed marriage, you may need to get a special dispensation and arrange to have religious instruction before your wedding.

In any case, you'll need to confirm your wedding date with the clergyman — or, of course, with any civil authority who will be officiating at a nonreligious ceremony — to make sure he will be available. In large or popular churches and halls, it's often necessary to reserve your date and time several months in advance.

Once the date is set, your clergyman will explain the details of the marriage ceremony — whether you use a standard text or write your own service — and clarify rules on music, photographs and decorations. If you'd like to have another clergyman — perhaps a relative, chaplain or family friend — participate in the ceremony, you'll need permission. Whether the visiting clergyman performs the entire ceremony or merely assists the pastor, it's customary to give the usual fee to both.

Once you've settled all the details with your clergyman, it's a good idea to arrange to see the sexton or secretary. If you plan to have a candlelight ceremony, for example, he can explain the fire laws and show you what the church provides in the way of candelabra. It's his business to know all about aisle carpets, prayer benches, canopies and any other special equipment you might need. He can also advise you on reserved parking spaces and make the necessary arrangements for your rehearsal.

The church organist is also an important person to see before your wedding. You'll need to know exactly what musical selections are allowed and what the organist recommends before you arrange your musical program. Also, you'll want the organist at your wedding rehearsal, for music plays an important part in the pacing of the wedding ceremony. If a soloist will sing, schedule several rehearsals. (For some musical selections, see Chapter X.)

YOUR MARRIAGE LICENSE

All states require a marriage license, filled out by the clergyman and signed by witnesses the day of the wedding. Apply together for your license at the city clerk's office two to three weeks before your wedding. You will need proof that you are of age or that you have your parents' consent to marry and proof of citizenship if you were not born in the United States. And you will both need doctor's certificates verifying the results of your blood tests and physical examinations. There is usually a waiting period (perhaps two to three days) to get the results, and the certificate is good for a maximum time limit (usually about thirty days). Keep this limit and the valid period of your marriage license (usually thirty days) in mind when you make a date to get the license. Your groom pays the fee.

SELECTING YOUR RINGS

The bride's wedding band may be chosen to match her engagement ring or to be worn beautifully alone. It may or may not match her husband's. If you want your rings engraved, you may choose the traditional inscription of the bride's maiden initials, the groom's initials and the wedding date, in that order. For example, "R. G. S. from J. R. B. 6/12/73." Or you may inscribe any sentimental phrase that fits in the space available. If you plan to have a double ring ceremony, your maid of honor will hold the groom's ring and the best man will hold yours until they are actually exchanged.

WHO PAYS FOR WHAT?

The bride's family is entirely responsible for the wedding ceremony; and in most cases they bear the complete cost of the reception as well. In some cases, however, the groom's family may offer to share in the cost of the reception, and the bride's family may accept if they wish. Naturally it is unwise, as well as in poor taste, for either family to go into debt paying for a wedding beyond their means. Otherwise, wedding costs are traditionally divided as follows:

THE BRIDE OR HER FAMILY PAYS FOR

Invitations and announcements.
Bride's wedding dress, veil and accessories.

Bride's trousseau.

Bouquets for the maid of honor, bridesmaids and flower girl.

Flowers for the ceremony and reception.

Engagement and wedding photographs.

Rental fee for the church or hall.

Fees for the sexton, organist and soloist.

Rental of aisle carpet, canopy and other equipment.

Transportation of the bridal party to the ceremony and reception.

Complete reception, including all food, beverages, music, decorations and professional services, unless the groom's family offers to assume some of this expense.

Groom's wedding ring.

Groom's wedding gift.

Gifts for the bride's attendants.

Lodging for bridesmaids from out of town.

Bride's personal writing paper.

THE GROOM OR HIS FAMILY PAYS FOR

Bride's engagement and wedding rings.

Marriage license.

Clergyman's fee (ranging from $10 to $100).

Bride's bouquet and going-away flowers (see below).

Boutonnières for the men of the wedding party.

Flowers for the mothers and grandmothers (see below).

Gloves and ties (or ascots) for the men of the wedding party.

Bride's wedding gift.

Gifts for the best man and ushers.

Lodging for ushers from out of town.

Complete wedding trip.

OPTIONAL EXPENSES USUALLY SET BY LOCAL CUS-
TOM:

Bride's bouquet — traditionally a gift from the groom,
but may be included in the bridal outfit supplied by her
family.

Flowers for mothers and grandmothers — usually provided
by the groom, but the bride may buy those for her own
mother and grandmothers.

Attendants' dresses — usually bought by each girl, but
the bride may provide them if she chooses.

Bridesmaids' party — usually given by the bride, but may
be given by her attendants or relatives.

Bachelor party — given by the groom's attendants and
friends in most places, but may also be given by the
groom.

Rehearsal dinner — given by the groom's family in most
communities, but may also be hosted by relatives or
friends of the bride.

BRIDE'S REMINDER LIST

You'll need about six months to arrange your wedding.
If you are planning a very small wedding, you may postpone
or eliminate some of the usual preparations, but it's best to
get everything done as soon as possible.

SIX MONTHS before your wedding:

Select your wedding date and set the time of the ceremony.

Discuss your budget with your parents and decide what type of wedding you will have.

Decide where your wedding and reception will take place.

Determine the number of guests you can accommodate and start making out your guest list. Have your fiancé start making out his. Remember that guests must be invited to ceremony and reception when both are held in the same place.

Make arrangements to visit the clergyman or other officiating authority with your fiancé.

Plan your reception and make the necessary arrangements with the caterer, florist, musicians and others involved.

Begin to choose your wedding dress, veil and accessories. Since wedding dresses are usually made to order, allow a minimum of two months for delivery.

Select your china, silver, glassware and other household items, and register your choices with your favorite store.

Discuss with your fiancé how many attendants you'll have and begin to choose. Keep in mind any religious rules about who may serve as your attendants.

Start planning your new home and begin your household shopping, paying for purchases out of your own money or money you receive as gifts.

Begin shopping for your trousseau.

Invite your attendants to order their dresses and headpieces.

Discuss honeymoon plans with your fiancé so he can make the necessary reservations. If you plan to leave the country, you'll have to check on passports, visas and shots.

THREE MONTHS before your wedding:

Complete your guest list and check it for duplications with your fiancé's.

Read Chapter V carefully, then order your invitations, announcements and enclosure cards. Engraving usually takes three to four weeks.

Get the envelopes in advance and begin addressing them so they'll be ready for mailing as soon as you receive the invitations.

Order your personal writing paper. (See the section on thank-you notes in Chapter XV.)

Discuss your wedding color scheme with both mothers so they can order their dresses.

Engage a photographer and arrange for your bridal portrait. (See Chapter XIV.)

Discuss the ceremony details with the proper authorities.

Arrange all your reception details with the person in charge.

Make an appointment for a physical examination.

ONE MONTH before your wedding:

Mail your invitations. Record acceptances and regrets as they arrive. Send out maps and pew cards, if needed, to those who accept.

Order all the flowers (including boutonnières and flowers to wear for the ceremony and reception). (See Chapter XIII.)

Have the final fitting of your dress and headpiece.

Have your wedding portrait made.

Arrange to have your attendants' dresses fitted.

Choose and order the gifts for your attendants.

Order the groom's wedding ring.

Select a wedding gift for the groom.

Order your wedding cake if it's not included in the catering service.

Arrange accomodations for relatives and attendants from
out of town.

Make arrangements for the bridesmaids' party if you're
giving one.

Discuss arrangements for the rehearsal dinner with the
hostess.

Write thank-you notes for all gifts as they arrive.

Check with your newspaper for details on the wedding
announcement, then prepare it accordingly.

TWO WEEKS before your wedding:

Make an appointment with your hairdresser.

Go with your fiancé to get the marriage license.

Complete your trousseau purchases.

Arrange transportation of the bridal party to the ceremony.
A limousine is customary for the bride, but private cars
may be used for other members of the group.

Discuss details of the wedding and reception with your
candid photographer.

Check on the delivery of all purchases.

Deliver your wedding announcement and photograph to
the newspapers.

ONE WEEK before your wedding:

Begin your honeymoon packing.

Make sure your announcements are ready to mail after the
ceremony.

Arrange the wedding rehearsal and see that each member

of the wedding party is informed of the date, time and place.

Present gifts to your attendants at the bridesmaids' party or the rehearsal dinner.

Check on final details with your florist, photographer and others providing professional services.

Arrange to have your wedding gifts and personal belongings moved to your new home.

Keep up with your thank-you letters.

GROOM'S REMINDER LIST

The groom doesn't have nearly so many wedding preparations to make as the bride, but his responsibilities are important ones. Those listed below are spaced over a six-month period — the time that is needed to arrange a formal wedding.

SIX MONTHS before the wedding:

Order your bride's wedding and engagement rings.

Make out your guest list and turn it over to your fiancée.

Make arrangements with your fiancée to visit the clergyman.

Discuss with your fiancée the number of ushers you'll need (about one for each fifty guests).

Discuss honeymoon plans with your bride and start making the necessary reservations. If you're leaving the country, check on passports, visas and inoculations.

THREE MONTHS before the wedding:

Consult your fiancée on wedding clothes and order yours.
Invite your best man and ushers to participate and brief
them on the proper attire.
Complete plans for your wedding trip and purchase the
necessary tickets.

ONE MONTH before the wedding:

Make an appointment for your blood test and physical
examination.

TWO WEEKS before the wedding:

Make a date with your bride-to-be to get the marriage
license.
Check on the arrangements for your bachelor dinner if
you're having one.
Arrange with your best man for transportation from the
reception to the airport or wherever you plan to embark
on your honeymoon.

ONE WEEK before the wedding:

Remind your best man and ushers of the rehearsal and
rehearsal dinner.
Present gifts to your attendants at the bachelor dinner or
rehearsal dinner.
Brief the head usher on any special seating arrangements.
Put the minister's fee in a sealed envelope and give it to the

best man. (He will give it to the minister.)
Get your going-away clothes in order so you can change at
the reception.
Pack for your honeymoon.

5
Your Invitations and Announcements

THE WORDING OF wedding invitations and announcements is traditionally set by etiquette, as are the paper and engraving. This is not to say that a talented designer might not have informal invitations printed in an original style; in fact, some fine specialty stores do offer unusual papers, inks and styles as a custom service. But for a formal wedding, it is best to stay with the traditional invitation format.

THE GUEST LIST

After you and your family decide how many guests you wish to invite to your wedding, ask your fiancé's mother to give you her list. You should specify how many guests you want your fiancé's family to invite; usually this number is half the total guest list, but in special circumstances, one family may have a longer list than the other. If your fiancé's parents are divorced, the invitation privilege belongs to the parent with whom he lives, but he should make sure that no one — particularly none of his grandparents — to whom the wedding is important is omitted except for compelling reasons.

If you are planning a very large wedding, you'll want to include everyone to whom your wedding will be meaningful. Old address and telephone books, alumni directories, Christmas card lists, club lists are all helpful in making certain that no one is forgotten.

Do send invitations to your clergyman and his wife, all of your fiancé's immediate family, the members of your wedding party and their parents, even though they've been invited informally. It is unnecessary to include escorts for single guests on your list. If you want to invite the friend or fiancé of a friend of yours, ask for the escort's name and address and send him an invitation.

At this same time, you should compile your announcement list, including all those acquaintances with whom you wish to share the good news of your marriage. It is most gracious to send invitations to everyone you would like to have with you, even those you know will not be able to attend. Neither a wedding invitation nor an announcement requires a gift, so you may send them shamelessly to everyone who will want to share your joy.

Send your fiancé's mother three or four unsealed invitations as soon as they are ready. These keepsakes may be accompanied by a note from your mother mentioning the date when the others will be mailed.

PAPER AND ENGRAVING

Although handwritten invitations may be sent to twenty-five or fewer guests for a small ceremony, for a formal wedding, you will want formal invitations. These are engraved on the top page of a double sheet of white or off-white plain or paneled paper of the best quality you can afford. Each invitation has two envelopes — the inner one encloses the invitation or announcement and accompanying cards, and the outer one is addressed and stamped.

The type of engraving is largely a matter of personal choice, but here are some of the most popular styles:

Solid Antique Roman

Linear Modified Roman

SHADED ROMAN

Shaded Antique Roman

Norman

London Script

English Script

Order your invitations from a jeweler, a stationer, a department store or a bridal salon at least two months before the ceremony to allow time for engraving, addressing and mailing. When you order, have the envelopes sent in advance so you may have them addressed and ready. Be sure to order a few extras in case you make mistakes.

ADDRESSING

Make up a master list (if you put it on cards, you'll have no trouble alphabetizing and eliminating duplications), making sure that all names and titles are spelled correctly. Address all invitations by hand, never by typewriter. You may address them yourself, ask your bridesmaids to help or have a special service do them for you.

The outside envelope, the one to be sealed, is addressed to

> *Mr. and Mrs. James Wallace McDermott*
> *1088 Fielding Avenue*
> *Metropolis, Ohio 12345*

The only abbreviations used are Mr., Mrs. and Dr.

The unsealed inner envelope does not include first names or addresses, but reads simply

> *Mr. and Mrs. McDermott*

If several members of a family are to be invited, avoid using the phrase "and family." Young children may be mentioned on the inside envelope as

Mr. and Mrs. McDermott
Elaine and Charles

Adult members of a family should receive separate invitations, whether they still live with their parents or not. If two sisters or two brothers live at the same address, however, you may send one invitation to both. The outside envelope reads.

Miss Barbara McDermott
Miss Elaine McDermott

or

Mr. Robert McDermott
Mr. Charles McDermott

On the inside envelope of an invitation to two sisters, write "The Misses McDermott," and to two brothers put "The Messrs. McDermott." In either case, omit "The" if you prefer.

Two unrelated friends living together as roommates each get an invitation.

MAILING

First the larger, more formal invitation is folded across the middle of the engraved double sheet, then placed in the inner envelope with the fold down. On opening, a guest should first see the names of the bride's parents. The less formal invitation is not folded again, but is placed in the envelope in its original size with the engraved side facing up.

Extra enclosures — pew cards, reception cards, at home cards — may be placed next to the engraving or be inserted in one fold of the invitation or announcement. Tissues placed over the lettering to prevent smudging may be left in place for mailing. If they are not inserted by the engraver, however, there is no need to add them.

The unsealed inner envelope is placed in the outer envelope so that the recipient's name comes immediately to view as the outside envelope is opened.

Mail invitations three to four weeks before the wedding to allow time for checking acceptances and notifying your caterer. Mail announcements the day of the wedding or as soon afterward as possible. If a return address is necessary, it is usually embossed colorlessly on the flap of the outer envelope.

THE WORDING OF YOUR INVITATIONS

Your parents should issue the invitations and announcements whether you are living at home or not. If your parents are not living, your guardian, closest relatives or family friends may sponsor the wedding and issue the invitations. If your parents are divorced, the parent with whom you live issues invitations and announcements.

On formal invitations, all names appear in full without nicknames. Spell out "Junior" if space permits. Spell out numbers, including those in short addresses. The date is written "*Saturday, the sixth of July*," with the year spelled out on the following line. You may omit the year from wed-

ding invitations. The time is written as *"four o'clock"* or
"half after four o'clock."

"The honour of your presence" is always requested for a religious ceremony, but *"the pleasure of your company"* is requested for the reception. You may request a reply to a reception invitation, using any of these phrases: *"R.S.V.P.,"*
"Please respond," "Kindly respond" or *"The favour of a reply is
requested."* Note that *honour* and *favour* are always spelled with
the "u."

The typical church wedding invitation reads:

> *Mr. and Mrs. Charles Morton Fine*
> *request the honour of your presence*
> *at the marriage of their daughter*
> *Susan Ann*
> *to*
> *Mr. David Mark Craig*
> *Saturday, the sixth of May*
> *at four o'clock*
> *All Saints' Church*
> *Barton, Texas*

The formal reception card to accompany the invitation
would read:

> *Mr. and Mrs. Charles Morton Fine*
> *request the pleasure of your company*
> *on Saturday, the sixth of May*
> *at half after four o'clock*
> *Glenn Hills Country Club*

R.S.V.P.
62 Laurel Lane
Barton, Texas

A joint reception card adds the groom's parents' names on a line below the bride's parents':

Mr. and Mrs. Charles Morton Fine
and
Mr. and Mrs. James Lincoln Craig
request the pleasure . . . etc.

The reception card may also take this simplified form:

Reception
immediately following the ceremony
Glenn Hills Country Club

Kindly respond
32 Laurel Lane
Barton, Texas

RECEPTION INVITATION: If the reception has a larger guest list than the ceremony, invitations are issued to the reception with ceremony cards enclosed. The invitation reads:

Mr. and Mrs. Charles Morton Fine
request the pleasure of your company
at the wedding reception of their daughter
Susan Ann
and
Mr. David Mark Craig
Saturday, the sixth of May

at half after four o'clock
Glenn Hills Country Club
Barton, Texas

Please respond
22 Laurel Lane
Barton, Texas

The joint invitation reads:

Mr. and Mrs. Charles Morton Fine
and
Mr. and Mrs. James Lincoln Craig
request the pleasure of your company
at the wedding reception of their children
Susan Ann
and
David Mark
Saturday, . . . etc.

The ceremony card reads:

Mr. and Mrs. Charles Morton Fine
request the honour of your presence
Saturday, the sixth of May
at four o'clock
All Saints' Church
Barton, Texas

The ceremony card may also take this simplified form:

Ceremony
at four o'clock
All Saints' Church

If there are too few guests invited to the ceremony to warrant special cards, send your family's informal note or card with the simple note handwritten over the engraved names, *"Ceremony at four o'clock. All Saints' Church."* You may also send handwritten notes or simply tell your guests.

COMBINED INVITATION: If all guests are to be invited to both the ceremony and the reception, a combined invitation may be used without separate enclosure cards. It reads:

Mr. and Mrs. Charles Morton Fine
request the honour of your presence
at the marriage of their daughter
Susan Ann
to
Mr. David Mark Craig
Saturday, the sixth of May
at four o'clock
All Saints' Church
Barton, Texas
and afterwards at
Glenn Hills Country Club

Please respond
22 Laurel Lane
Barton, Texas

This form is not so formal as having separate enclosures,

and it does not permit the names of both sets of parents to appear.

INFORMAL INVITATION: Engraved invitations may be sent to a small informal wedding, but they are not necessary.

For a very small wedding to which only a few very close friends and relatives are to be invited, your mother should send out handwritten notes or invite guests personally at least two weeks before the ceremony. You or your friends may help her write the notes, but the notes must be sent in her name, and should be written in a natural style. Such a note might read:

Dear Helen,

Judy and Michael are to be married at half past four on Wednesday, the fifth of May, in the Lady Chapel of Grace Church here in Cedar Springs. It will be a small wedding with a reception afterward at our house. You know how much we want you to be with us on that day.

Affectionately,
Louise

It is always more gracious to write notes, but if necessary, you may telephone your invitations. If you telephone for your mother, you should say, "Mother wants me to invite you, . . . etc.," so that guests will know that your family is happy about your wedding.

SPECIAL INVITATIONS

WIDOWED PARENTS: If one of your parents has died, the wedding invitation takes the following form unless the widow or widower has remarried. A widow would send out an invitation reading:

> *Mrs. Randolph Clay Marshall*
> *requests the honour of your presence*
> *at the marriage of her daughter*
> *Mary Louise*
> etc.

A widower would substitute the expression *"his daughter."*

When the bride's mother has remarried, the relationship between the bride and her stepfather is clarified when this form is used:

> *Mr. and Mrs. Lansing Hoyt Lane*
> *request the honour of your presence*
> *at the marriage of Mrs. Lane's daughter*
> *Mary Louise Marshall*
> etc.

If the bride is very close to her stepfather, it is correct to use this form:

Mr. and Mrs. Lansing Hoyt Lane
request the honour of your presence
at the marriage of their daughter
Mary Louise Marshall
etc.

When the bride's father has remarried, the relation to her stepmother is shown by this form:

Mr. and Mrs. Donald Peabody Stewart
request the honour of your presence
at the marriage of Mr. Stewart's daughter
Karen Lynn
etc.

DIVORCED PARENTS: When the parents of the bride are divorced, the wedding invitation is usually issued by the parent with whom the bride lives. If you live with your mother and she has not remarried, the invitation reads:

Mrs. Smith Watson
requests the honour of your presence
at the marriage of her daughter
Mary Jane
etc.

Note that a divorced woman formally uses this combination of her maiden surname and her former husband's surname.
    If the bride's mother has remarried, she may use either of

the forms suggested for the remarried widow. The same rules apply when the invitation is issued by the bride's father, or in using the names of the groom's widowed, divorced or remarried parents. Invitations are always issued in the name of the host and hostess. Unless family relations are extraordinarily strained, the husband or wife of a remarried parent should never be omitted.

SPONSORS OTHER THAN PARENTS: If the bride is being sponsored by relatives other than her parents, the explanatory words *"his sister,"* *"her sister,"* or *"his,"* *"her"* or *"their niece"* are substituted for the phrase *"their daughter."* If the bride is being sponsored by close friends, the invitation indicates this by giving the bride's full name, prefaced by *"Miss."* Such an invitation might read

> *Mr. and Mrs. George Poe Donato*
> *request the honour of your presence*
> *at the marriage of*
> *Miss Adelaide Tate Burke*
> etc.

SPONSORLESS WEDDING: When a bride has no sponsor — no family or close friends nearby — she may correctly send out her own invitations. Such an invitation reads:

> *The honour of your presence*
> *is requested at the marriage of*
> *Miss Jane Michaels*
> *to*

Mr. Leo Williams
Saturday, the fifth of December
at four o'clock
Trinity Church
Marysville, Arkansas

This invitation might include the simplified form of the reception card shown on page 49 or card saying:

The pleasure of your company is requested
Saturday, the fifth of December
at half after four o'clock
The York Club
Marysville, Arkansas
R.S.V.P.
Ten Winton Lane
Marysville, Arkansas

SECOND MARRIAGE: When invitations for the second wedding of a widowed daughter are issued by the bride's parents, a formal invitation takes this form:

Mr. and Mrs. John Lewis Bruce
request the honour of your presence
at the marriage of their daughter
Linda Judith James   or *Linda James*
etc.

The invitation for a divorced bride reads:

Mr. and Mrs. John Lewis Bruce
request the honour of your presence
at the marriage of their daughter
Linda Bruce James
etc.

Note that a divorcée uses her maiden surname before her ex-husband's surname, while a widow uses only her given name or names. The prefix *Mrs.* is never used before a bride's name unless she issues her own invitations.

DOUBLE WEDDINGS: A formal invitation to a double wedding of sisters would read:

Mr. and Mrs. Robert Paul Bentley
request the honour of your presence
at the marriage of their daughters
Katherin Barbara
to
William Leon Shakespeare
and
Cynthia Jill
to
Steven Roger Mozart
on the evening of Saturday, the first of August
at nine o'clock
First Congregational Church
Clifton, Idaho

When the brides are not sisters, separate invitations may be sent by each family, or they may send a joint invitation. For example,

Mr. and Mrs. Jacob Catt Snow
and
Mr. and Mrs. Nero White
request the honour of your presence
at the marriage of their daughters
Agatha Catt Snow
to
Mr. Vincent Barge Bigley
and
Bianca White
to
Mr. Bartholomew Donalds
etc.

SPECIAL ENCLOSURES

AT HOME CARDS: At home cards may be enclosed with invitations, but are more often used with announcements. They always include the couple's new address and the date on which it became effective. A typical at home cards reads:

At home
after the twenty-sixth of August
1413 Fountain Avenue
Glendale, Wyoming

When enclosed with announcements, they may also take this form:

Mr. and Mrs. John Simon Eagle
after the tenth of April
1035 Fifth Avenue
New York

CEREMONY CARDS: When there is any chance that un-invited persons may try to attend the ceremony, engraved cards may be enclosed with invitations to be presented at the door for admittance. These are used only for very formal weddings, usually of prominent persons, and read:

Please present this card
St. Martin's Church
Saturday, the fifth of April

PEW CARDS: Pew cards are used when special seating arrangements have been made for relatives and very close friends. They are best sent after the acceptance has been received to ensure the correct number of reserved seats, but they may be enclosed with the invitation and a chance taken that the guest will decline. They may take several forms. The simplest is the bride's mother's personal calling card with a handwritten pew number in the lower lefthand corner. A more elaborate form reads:

Please present this card
St. Martin's Church
Saturday, the fifth of April
Pew number *9*

The third form is a combination of handwritten and engraved:

Mr. and Mrs. John Shine
will please present this card to an usher
at Saint Martin's Church
Pew number *9*

General reservations may be indicated by the use of the phrase "within the ribbons" on either of the first two cards in place of the special pew number. This may be handwritten or engraved. However, these cards are used only for very formal weddings.

MILITARY AND OTHER TITLES

"Mr." precedes the name of the bride's father and that of the groom on invitations unless they are clergyman, physicians, high officials or members of the armed forces on active duty. A clergyman's full title — The Reverend, Bishop, Rabbi — is spelled out in full before his name. The name of a medical doctor is preceded by "Dr." instead of "Mr." When the bride or her mother is a physician, however, the title is usually omitted, unless other circumstances indicate that the mother would not use her husband's name, or that the bride would otherwise be titled "Miss," as when friends issue her invitations. The titles of Senators, judges and other high officials may be used, but those of lesser officials are omitted.

The use of military titles on invitations is subject to changing regulations and should always be verified with the commanding officer. Usually, however, the title of the bride's father is spelled out in front of his name. The groom's title is used before his name only if he holds a rank equivalent to or higher than Captain in the Army or Commander in the Navy. If he holds a lesser rank, it is usually listed with his branch of service, as follows:

Jeffrey Ronald Sherman
Lieutenant, United States Army

If the groom is an enlisted man, his branch of service may be listed without mention of his rank. In either case, however, the "Mr." is omitted. Reserve officers do not use military titles unless they are on active duty. A bride in military service follows the same rules as a groom.

RECALLING INVITATIONS

If a formal wedding must be postponed or cancelled after the invitations have gone out, all invited guests must be notified as soon as possible. When time permits, this is properly done with engraved or printed cards. If there has been a death in the family, the cards would read:

Mrs. James Alan Roberts
regrets that the death of
Mr. Roberts
obliges her to recall the invitations
to the wedding of her daughter
Saturday, the seventh of April

An invitation recalled in this manner indicates only that the ceremony will not take place as originally planned. When a death or serious illness in the family renders a large wedding inappropriate, the marriage may still take place as a small family ceremony. The couple may wear their formal wedding attire, but usually only a maid of honor and a best man attend them.

If the wedding is merely postponed, this fact is usually indicated on the notification card. If the wedding is cancelled, however, no reason need be given. A cancellation card would read:

Mr. and Mrs. James Alan Roberts
announce that the marriage of
their daughter
Virginia
to
Mr. David Martin Andrews
will not take place.

If time is short, invitations may be recalled by personal

notes, telegrams or telephone calls. Notes should be patterned after the cards, signed by the person who issued the invitations and calls made in the name of the bride's mother. Reasons other than a death or illness in the family are not usually mentioned.

HOW TO WORD YOUR ANNOUNCEMENTS

Send announcements only to persons who are not invited to the wedding. Most often used following an elopement, announcements may be sent if limited facilities prohibit you from sending invitations to all the friends and relatives you'd like to inform of your marriage.

The engraving and paper for announcements is the same as that for invitations. Announcements should be addressed just as wedding invitations are, and, whenever possible, should be ready to mail immediately after the ceremony. In any case, they are mailed at the earliest possible date.

A typical announcement reads:

Mr. and Mrs. William Charles Benton
have the honour of announcing
the marriage of their daughter
Deirdre
to
Mr. James Lawrence Bowles
on Friday, the tenth of May
One thousand nine hundred and seventy-three
Trinity Methodist Church
Portland, Oregon

The bride's parents may also *"have the honour to announce the marriage"* or simply *"announce the marriage."* The date, year and city in which the marriage took place are always included on an announcement. The actual site of the ceremony, however, need not be mentioned.

When the bride or her parents are divorced or widowed, the wording is varied in the same manner indicated for invitations. If you have no parents or close relatives to issue the announcements, you and your groom may issue your own. Also correct for mature or previously married brides, such an announcement would read:

Miss Deirdre Benton
and
Mr. James Lawrence Bowles
announce their marriage
Friday, the tenth of May
One thousand nine hundred and seventy-three
Scarsdale, New York

6
Who's Who
in the Wedding Party

A WEDDING PARTY is aptly named, for these are the people most intimately associated with the happy celebration of your marriage. They are

THE BRIDE

You have a great many preparations to make for your day in the limelight. Your fiancé, parents, relatives and friends will aid and advise you, of course, but the ultimate responsibility for the plans and arrangements is yours. After giving careful consideration to your budget and the wishes of your groom and your parents, you must decide exactly what kind of wedding and reception you'll have, and when and where they will be. Once these decisions are made, it's up to you to see that all the plans are carried out.

As soon as you've set the style, date and place of your wedding and reception (See Chapter IV), you and your fiancé should visit the clergyman to confirm the date and settle the ceremony details. It's also important to start making out your guest lists, taking care to avoid disappointments and wounded feelings. When the list is complete, your invitations, announcements and enclosure cards must be ordered. (See Chapter V.) Start addressing your invitations early enough to have them ready to mail at least three weeks before your wedding. Select your bridal outfit well in advance to allow time for fittings and photographs.

One of the most pleasant privileges of being a bride is choosing the friends who will be your attendants. It's also your prerogative to choose the dresses they'll wear, but it's nice to let them make the final selection from several you like. To show your appreciation to your attendants, you give each one a small gift as a memento of the occasion. This might be a pair of gloves to wear in the wedding, a silver compact, a bracelet engraved with the wedding date or some other personal item. You may entertain for your bridesmaids as well, but that's up to you. Another optional custom you'll probably want to follow is that of exchanging wedding gifts with your groom. Almost anything you know he'd like, from a wristwatch to a piece of fine luggage, is suitable. The last (but not the least) of your responsibilities is the acknowledgement of your wedding gifts. You must write a personal note of appreciation for each and every gift you receive. The notes need not be long, but they should be prompt. The best procedure is to write a few each day so you don't get behind. (For more details on thank you notes, see Chapter XV.)

If you prepare carefully, you can relax and enjoy your wedding day. You can float down the aisle on a cloud of white, greet all your reception guests with a happy smile, then dash off on your honeymoon with a carefree wave.

THE GROOM

After you've set the date, your groom's first responsibility is to compile his guest list within the limits set by your family. He'll include the people his parents want to ask, of course. The groom is privileged to choose his best man and ushers, and may also entertain them if he likes. He makes sure his attendants are informed about proper dress for the wedding, and presents each of them with a small gift — monogrammed jewelry, cigarette lighters or key chains, perhaps.

You may help pick out your wedding ring, but your groom buys it and has it engraved. He may also buy you a special wedding gift — anything you want except clothes, a house or a car. The groom assumes responsibility for getting the marriage license and any other necessary documents, and he makes all the arrangements for your wedding trip.

On the wedding day, your groom's primary concern is to get to the ceremony on time. (His best man will take care of everything else.) He accepts the congratulations of the guests in the receiving line, responds to the toasts, then takes you away with him for a happy honeymoon.

THE MAID OF HONOR

Your maid or matron of honor should be someone who is very close to you — perhaps your sister if she is the right age. You might also choose a dear friend, your favorite cousin or your sister-in-law. You needn't ask your fiancé's sister to be your honor attendant unless she happens to be a very close friend of yours. If you have two sisters or close friends and one of them is married, you may have both a maid and a matron of honor, but you must designate one of them to handle the official duties. Usually the maid is given precedence — walking down the aisle immediately before the bride and being seated in a position of honor at the reception.

The honor attendant has no definite pre-wedding responsibilities, but is expected to help the bride as much as possible. She might help address the invitations, for example, or she might take charge of recording and displaying your wedding gifts. If there are several bridesmaids, the maid of honor might arrange to have their dresses fitted and see that each is properly attired and at the church on time. She assembles her own wedding outfit, paying for everything except her flowers. She attends all of the pre-wedding parties in your honor and may give one herself. At a home wedding, the honor attendant is the one who greets the clergyman and shows him where to change.

The maid of honor is usually one of the two official witnesses required by law to sign the marriage certificate. She precedes you and your father down the aisle, arranges your train and veil and holds your bouquet during the ceremony. She stands next to the groom in the receiving line and sits on his left at the bridal table. Once the receiving line is completed, she is free to enjoy the reception as an honored guest, but she may take time out to help you change into your going away outfit and to bid you a fond farewell.

THE BEST MAN

This responsible role is usually filled by the groom's most trustworthy friend or relative. His brother, if he has one of appropriate age, is the most logical choice, but a good friend or a cousin is equally suitable. In fact, the groom may properly choose any adult male — including his own father — to be his best man.

The duties of the best man are many and varied. He's the indispensable chief of staff at the wedding, toastmaster at the reception and personal valet and adviser to the groom. It's his responsibility to see that the groom is properly dressed at the church at the appointed time. There he sticks close to his side, lending him moral and physical support as needed. The best man takes charge of the marriage license (which he signs as an official witness) and the bride's wedding ring, producing each at the proper time. He takes the minister's fee from the groom and presents it to the clergyman in a sealed envelope at the first opportune moment. He may also supervise the ushers, making sure that all are uniformly dressed, thoroughly briefed and at the ceremony site at the appointed time.

Although the best man does not participate in the receiving line, he does have a number of reception responsibilities. He sits to the right of the bride and proposes the first toast to the new couple. This is usually a wish for health, happiness and prosperity, and may be worded any way he likes. After the toasts, he collects all the congratulatory telegrams and reads them aloud if the bride and groom wish. He makes sure that the reception runs smoothly and that no practical jokes are played on the bride and groom.

The best man's final responsibility is to get the newlyweds off to a smooth start on their honeymoon. He helps the groom change into his going away clothes (the next day he may take all the rental clothes back to the outfitter) and may assist with last-minute packing. He takes charge of the luggage, seeing that it is safely locked in the honeymoon car or checked ahead at the station or airport. When you and your groom leave the reception, the best man will help you into your getaway car or drive you to the station or airport. Then, as you make your departure, he will hand over the keys, tickets and baggage checks given to him for safe-keeping.

THE BRIDESMAIDS

The number of bridesmaids you'll have in your wedding depends on its size and style. You might have a small wedding with no bridesmaids at all, or a large formal wedding with as many as twelve. It is the bride's prerogative to choose her attendants from among her closest friends and relatives of appropriate age. If you have young sisters or cousins between the ages of thirteen and sixteen, they can participate as junior bridesmaids. It's also customary to ask at least one relative of the groom — his sister or a favorite cousin, perhaps — to be a bridesmaid. Even if she is your sister or dearest friend, however, a girl who is pregnant should not be asked to be in the wedding party.

Although bridesmaids have no specific pre-wedding duties, they usually offer to run errands, address envelopes and help the bride in any way they can. They are invited to all the pre-wedding parties and may give one if they wish. Bridesmaids are responsible for assembling and paying for their own wedding outfits, but they must dress uniformly. They receive their flowers when they gather at your home an hour or so before the ceremony; or you may have their flowers delivered directly to the site of the ceremony. Bridesmaids always take part in the wedding processional and usually stand at the bride's side during the ceremony. They take turns standing in the receiving line and sit alternately with the ushers at the bride's table. They take part in all the reception festivities and are usually in the front ranks when the bride throws her bouquet.

THE USHERS

Ushers seat the guests at the ceremony and act as escorts for the bridesmaids. There should be an usher for every bridesmaid in the wedding party, as it's customary for them to pair off in the recessional. To avoid seating delays, there should be at least one usher for each fifty guests. Your groom might ask his brothers, brothers-in-law, cousins and best friends, whether married or single, to act in this capacity. He should also include any brothers or close relatives of yours who are the right age.

The ushers usually attend all the pre-wedding parties to which the groom is invited and may give one if they wish. They are obliged to provide their own wedding clothes. If they don't own the formal attire proper for the occasion, they may rent it. Your wedding party will look smarter if all their outfits come from one source — perhaps coordinated by the best man. The boutonnières, gloves and neckwear are usually provided by the groom.

Ushers arrive at the church, synagogue, hall or hotel forty-five minutes to an hour before the ceremony is set to begin and assemble near the entrance. As the guests arrive, an usher steps forward and offers his right arm to each woman. If she doesn't present a pew card and he doesn't know her, he asks if she is a friend of the bride or the groom. The bride's friends and relatives are seated on the left side of the church, the groom's on the right. If the church becomes too crowded on one side, however, late-arriving guests may be seated in the best available seats. When a man and a woman arrive together, the woman takes the arm of an usher, and the man follows them down the aisle. If several women arrive together, the eldest is seated first. A man alone may be accompanied to his seat by an usher. Ushers are expected to make polite conversation (in low tones, of course) with guests as they walk unhurriedly down the aisle.

The groom usually designates a head usher to supervise special seating arrangements. If one of the ushers is the brother of the bride or the groom, he will probably escort his own mother to her seat; otherwise the head usher assumes responsibility for the mothers. If an aisle carpet or pew ribbons are used, the groom appoints two ushers to take care of unrolling them. (See Chapter VIII.) Ushers participate in both the procession and the recessional, then return to escort the mothers and other honored guests from the church. Ushers do not stand in the receiving line, but they do sit at the bridal table. They often propose additional toasts to the happiness of the bride and groom. Throughout most of the reception, however, they just circulate and make sure that all the guests — especially the bridesmaids — have fun.

CHILD ATTENDANTS

Children add a lot of charm to a formal wedding, but they may also steal the show. To minimize the possibility of an intrusion upon the solemnity of your ceremony, you should limit your wedding party to one or two well-behaved children. The duties of flower girls, ring and train bearers and pages are best performed by brothers, sisters and other close relatives between the ages of four and eight.

The flower girl is the most popular child attendant. She may walk alone, with the ring bearer or with another flower girl about the same size, but she always comes immediately before the bride in the procession. It's traditional for a flower girl to carry a basket of loose petals to strew in the bride's path, but the danger of slipping on the petals has prompted some authorities to prohibit the practice. You may prefer to have your flower girl carry a tiny nosegay, a basket full of flowers or a flower-covered muff. In any case see that her flowers are the same back and front, so she can't hold them wrong.

The ring bearer carries a white satin pillow with the bride's ring (preferably not the real one) tied to the center with ribbons. After the ceremony, the cushion is turned upside down so the dummy ring won't show. Although he may be paired with a flower girl, he usually walks alone in the procession.

Pages or trainbearers always come in pairs about the same size. They are usually little boys, but girls occasionally serve in this capacity. You will not need pages, of course, unless your dress has a long train for them to carry.

Child attendants must attend the rehearsal so they can practice their parts, but they have no other duties. They do not attend pre-wedding parties and are often excused from the reception as well.

THE BRIDE'S MOTHER

Your mother helps you compile the guest list, arrange the details of the ceremony and reception and select your wedding outfit and trousseau. She may also keep track of your gifts, seeing that they are safely out of the way and attractively displayed. It's your mother's responsibility to keep your father and the groom's parents posted on the progress of the wedding plans. She and your fiancé's mother should confer on wedding attire so their dresses won't clash when they stand together in the receiving line.

Your mother is the official hostess for your wedding. She is privileged to sit in the very first pew on the bride's side of the aisle. She is the last person to be escorted to her seat before the wedding and the first to be ushered out after it's over. When she is hostess for the reception, she greets all the guests at the head of the receiving line, and sits in the place of honor at the parents' table. When you are ready to leave the reception, your mother should be granted a few minutes alone with you to say goodbye.

THE BRIDE'S FATHER

Your father has the privilege of riding to the ceremony with you in the limousine, and of escorting you down the aisle. After giving you away, he joins your mother in the first row. As the official host of the reception, he usually mingles with the guests instead of standing in the receiving line. He's the last person to leave the reception, and the one who bids the guests goodbye. Since your father's part is a prominent one, it's important for his dress to conform to that of your groom and the other men in the wedding party.

If your father is not living, you may ask your brother, your uncle or another male relative to give you away. If you have no such relative available, a good friend or an usher may escort you down the aisle. Your mother may then give you away.

If your parents are divorced, your father may still give you away. Instead of sitting with your mother, however, he would sit in the third row on the bride's side of the aisle.

THE GROOM'S PARENTS

Although the role played by the groom's parents is smaller than that of your parents, they should not be pushed into the background. Your fiancé's mother should be invited to all the showers, and both of his parents should be included at the rehearsal dinner. In some communities, it's customary for the groom's parents to give the rehearsal dinner. Your fiancé's parents contribute to the guest list for the wedding and reception. They consult with your parents on the proper wedding attire and dress accordingly. The groom's parents are the honored guests at the wedding and are seated just before your mother in the first pew on the groom's side of the aisle. The groom's mother always stands in the receiving line to greet the guests but his father's participation is optional.

SPECIAL MEMBERS OF THE WEDDING

If your wedding party is not large enough to include all of your favorite relatives or if you have brothers or sisters who are not the right age to participate in an official capacity, you may give them other duties. Young boys, for example, might light candles, distribute Mass books or *yarmulkes*, give out packets of rice or serve as acolytes. Girls might keep the bride's book or assist in serving refreshments at the reception.

Occasionally someone the bride wants to participate in the wedding must use crutches or a wheelchair. If your groom or either of your parents is in this situation, he or she should certainly play the traditional role in the service, with only such modifications as make entering or leaving the site of the ceremony as easy as possible. Other handicapped friends or relatives who might otherwise be asked to act as attendants might better be asked to take on some of the special duties suggested above.

7
Guide to Wedding Dress

THE CLOTHES YOU and the members of your wedding party wear set the style of the wedding. You may fall in love with a dress and plan a wedding around it, or you may set your time and place first, then shop for an appropriate outfit.

Styles of wedding dress change along with other fashions, but custom and convention continue to woo brides year after year. White has been worn in weddings for centuries and will probably continue to be worn for many years in all the flattering shades: candlelight, ivory, ecru, cream as well as snow white. The bridal veil is traditional and an important part of those religious ceremonies that require the bride's face to be covered. The clothes worn by the groom and the other men in the wedding party follow a traditional pattern that has been virtually the same for generations.

Your dress sets the style of the wedding and everyone else

dresses accordingly. The suggestions here represent accepted traditional formal wear. With greater availability of a wider range of styles in men's wear, your groom may choose a more current look for the men in the wedding party so long as it complements your dress. Bridesmaids have a little more latitude, but their dresses, too, must be in harmony with yours. Naturally the mothers of the bride and groom choose attire that conforms to the style of the wedding. Proper dress varies with the hour and the season as well as taste, and the wedding party should always dress consistently. Every usher should dress like the best man; each bridesmaid wears a style like that of the honor attendant; and both mothers appear in dresses of the same length and formality.

VERY FORMAL WEDDINGS

You'll look most magnificent in a stately dress of satin, lace, peau de soie or some equally formal fabric. It may be an heirloom dress worn with pride by generations of brides in your family, or it may be an elegant new design that simply suits you better than it could anyone else. No matter what makes you choose the particular style, however, a very formal dress should have a long train, like a cathedral length train. Such wedding dresses are always worn with a full veil, which may make up part of the train. You'll probably carry an elaborate bouquet or flower-trimmed prayer book and wear classically simple shoes to match your dress. Jewelry is optional, but any you wear should be simple and good. You may wear your engagement ring on your right hand until after the ceremony, when you may return it to your left hand. Keep in mind, however, that a ring on your right hand may prove painful when you shake hands in the receiving line.

The groom and all the other men in your wedding party wear formal clothes, which they may rent, if necessary. Everyone, including your father, dresses alike, but the neck-wear and boutonnières may be varied slightly to distinguish the groom and best man from the other men. For ceremonies starting before six o'clock in the evening, formal daytime wear consists of black or oxford gray cutaway coat, gray and black striped trousers, gray waistcoat, and formal white shirt with a wing collar. Accessories include a striped silk ascot with a pearl or gold stickpin, gray gloves, black shoes and black socks. Ushers sometimes wear starched, turned-down collars with striped four-in-hand ties in place of the wing collars and ascots worn by the groom and his best man. Gray spats and black silk top hats are also correct.

After six o'clock, the correct dress for your groom and his attendants is formal attire known as "white tie": a black tailcoat and matching satin-trimmed trousers, a white piqué waistcoat and a stiff-front shirt with a wing collar and French cuffs. Accessories include studs, a white piqué bow tie, white gloves, black patent leather pumps and long black socks. A black silk top hat is optional for all but the most formal weddings.

The bridesmaids and your maid or matron of honor wear elegant floor-length dresses in harmony with the line and feeling of your own dress. If you're wearing a classically simple satin empire, for example, choose a similar, unclut-tered style for your attendants. When it comes to the color scheme, choose whatever strikes your fancy, from an all-white wedding to one in rainbow hues. The maids usually wear identical dresses, but the honor attendant often wears a different shade or a contrasting color. She may carry flowers in a different color or style. Floral wreaths and ribbon head-bands, lace hats and wisps of veiling and three-cornered scarves all make attractive headpieces as long as they match or harmonize with the dresses. The bridesmaids in a very formal wedding always wear gloves to complement the length of their sleeves, although wrist-length white kid gloves are always correct, and often the most attractive. Their shoes should be simple and match the mood and color of their dresses. Attendants' jewelry is always uniform and usually quite simple.

Junior bridesmaids usually wear adaptations of the brides-maids' outfits. Their dresses are often made of the same color and fabric, styled along more youthful lines. Their flowers and headpieces may be identical to those of the other attend-ants, but ballet slippers are more suitable than high-heeled shoes for young girls.

Flower girls often wear floor-length dresses patterned after the bridesmaids' dresses, but almost any party dress is suit-able. A flower girl's outfit may be the same color as the bridesmaids' or she may wear a white dress trimmed or sashed in the matching color. A flower girl traditionally carries a basket of loose petals, but an old-fashioned nosegay of tiny flowers is much easier for a young child to handle. She also wears a simple floral or ribbon headband, white gloves and white or pastel ballet slippers or Mary Janes.

Ring bearers and pages may wear the satin and velvet suits once traditional. Or, if your little boys just don't feel at ease in such unconventional clothes, a good choice for any season is a dark blue Eton suit with short pants, a white shirt and either white or blue knee socks. For a summer wedding, a ring bearer might wear a white linen suit with white knee socks and white shoes. Young boys never wear formal attire patterned after that reserved for grown men. A small child in black tie looks lost in such clothes and is uncomfortable besides.

The mothers of the bride and groom always wear pretty, floor-length dinner or evening dresses to a very formal wedding. The styles may be less formal for a daytime ceremony than for one in the evening, but the length remains the same. Almost any flattering color — except all black or all white — is permissible, but it should be one that looks right with those worn by the rest of the wedding party. The mothers may wear small hats or veils, simple shoes and gloves and carry or wear flowers. If they take part in the ceremony, as in the Jewish service, the mothers entrust their handbags and wraps to a seated family member.

FORMAL WEDDINGS

You are every inch a bride in traditional, floor-length wedding dress with a short chapel or sweep train. A formal wedding dress may be a little less elaborate than that worn in a very formal wedding, and is often worn with a short veil, seldom longer than fingertip length. Lace mantillas and other headdresses are also appropriate for formal weddings. If the sleeves of your dress are not full length, you may wear gloves in white kid or in lace or fabric to match your dress. Your bouquet may be more simple than one you'd carry at a very formal wedding, but your shoes and all other accessories are the same.

The groom and other men in your wedding party dress according to the season and the hour of the ceremony. For a formal daytime wedding, the appropriate attire consists of a black or oxford gray sack coat or stroller (styled like a suit jacket), striped trousers, a gray waistcoat and a white shirt with a turned-down collar and French cuffs. These are customarily worn with a striped four-in-hand tie, gray gloves, black shoes and black socks. The proper hat is a Homburg, but this is frequently omitted.

For a formal ceremony starting after six o'clock in the evening, the men wear "black tie": a black dinner jacket with matching trousers, a white pleated-bosom shirt with a turned-down collar and French cuffs and a black vest or cummerbund. A black bow tie and black shoes and socks are the appropriate accessories. For a summer wedding, your groom could switch to a white dinner jacket, omit the gloves and wear a cummerbund in place of a vest.

The bridesmaids and maid or matron of honor dress in much the same manner for a formal wedding as they do for a very formal ceremony. Their dresses are usually floor-length, but not too ornate. Your attendants may wear shorter dresses if the wedding is relatively small and early in the day. Some type of headpiece is customary for a maid, but almost anything that complements her dress is suitable — simple ribbons or flowers, for example. Attendants' shoes may be dyed to match their dresses, and gloves are optional for a formal wedding.

Junior bridesmaids, flower girls and ring bearers are always attired in much the same fashion, no matter how formal the wedding. Children are usually omitted, however, at semiformal or informal ceremonies.

The mothers of the bride and groom usually wear long dinner dresses to a formal evening wedding, and street length costumes for daytime ceremonies. Either is correct as long as both mothers dress similarly.

Small hats or veils are customary for mothers at a church ceremony, but are optional when the wedding takes place at some other location. The guidelines for colors and other accessories are the same as those for mothers at a very formal wedding.

SEMIFORMAL WEDDINGS

You may wear an elaborate short dress or a simple floor-length dress without a train. If you wear a street-length dress, a short shoulder-length veil is best, but you may wear a veil reaching as far as your waist with a long dress. Your accessories, including your flowers, are simpler than those for a formal wedding.

The groom and his attendants usually wear solid dark suits with plain white shirts, four-in-hand ties and black shoes and long socks. For a summer wedding, the groom may be a little more casual and wear either a white linen jacket with oxford gray trousers or a dark blue jacket with gray or white flannel trousers.

The maid of honor and bridesmaids, if any, wear street-length dresses in harmony with that of the bride. Their shoes should complement their dresses. Attendants at a semiformal wedding may carry small bouquets or wear flowers. Gloves and hats are optional.

The mothers wear street-length attire similar to that of the maid of honor.

INFORMAL WEDDINGS

You'll wear street clothes for an informal wedding. You may choose any becoming color, fabric and style, but a suit in white or a color is customary. Accessories, which may be any color except black, include flowers to wear instead of a bouquet.

The groom and his best man wear the same conservative clothes appropriate for semiformal weddings.

The maid of honor dresses in much the same style as the bride.

The mothers also wear street clothes similar to that of the maid of honor.

8
Your Wedding Ceremony

THE CEREMONY IS what it's all about, after all, and should be planned with the greatest care. Discuss with your fiancé and your clergyman the significance of the vows you'll be reciting. Out of a careful reappraisal of tradition come the best innovations in all areas of human interaction. Add new prayers or poems, if you like, to make your ceremony perfectly express your feelings.

YOUR REHEARSAL

Your wedding rehearsal can not only give you and your attendants the opportunity to ensure that everything will go smoothly during the actual ceremony, it can also be the center of one of the many celebrations that may fill the weeks before your wedding. In addition to you and your fiancé, your father, the clergyman, the organist and all of your attendants should take part in the rehearsal. Each usher should be briefed on the proper procedure for seating guests before the ceremony, and those with special duties should be given complete instructions. If an aisle canvas and pew ribbons are to be used, two ushers are appointed and instructed in laying them.

The marriage service is not read at the rehearsal, but you and the clergyman will go over it, discussing any special variations you want made in the standard service (for example, you might want a special prayer or poem read) or to acquaint the clergyman with a service you two have written. He will point out any cues for your responses and outline the roles of the maid of honor and best man.

SEATING FOR THE CEREMONY

The first pew on the left side of the church is usually reserved for your parents, while that on the right is saved for your groom's. (These directions are reversed for Conservative and Orthodox Jewish weddings.) You may also reserve several additional pews on each side for other relatives and close family friends. This reserved section is usually indicated by special floral or ribbon markers on the aisle posts. "Within the ribbons" cards are sent to those you wish to honor with these special seats. All other guests are given the favored seats on the aisles and near the front as they arrive.

WEDDING TIME CHART

The amount of time necessary to get a wedding under way varies with the size and formality of the wedding, as well as with the distance to be traveled by each member of the bridal party. The following schedule is recommended for a large formal wedding taking place about fifteen minutes away from the bride's house.

Two hours before the ceremony, you begin dressing with your mother and your maid of honor lending assistance. If you and your attendants are dressing at the site of the ceremony, plan to arrive there at least an hour and a half before the ceremony.

One hour before the ceremony, the bridesmaids — all fully dressed — gather to pick up their flowers and pose for pictures. Although not essential, this allows you an opportunity to make sure that everyone is properly dressed. It also makes it possible for everyone to be transported to the ceremony in a group.

Forty-five to sixty minutes before the ceremony, the ushers arrive at the ceremony site and put on their boutonnières. They gather near the entrance to await the arrival of the first guests.

Thirty minutes before the ceremony, the organist begins the introductory music while the ushers escort guests to their

seats. Your friends and relatives are seated on the left side of
the church, your groom's on the right. (See Chapter VI.)

Twenty minutes before the ceremony, the groom and his best
man arrive. This is when the clergyman checks the marriage
license, receives his fee from the best man and issues any last
minute instruction he may find necessary.

Ten minutes before the ceremony, your maid of honor, bridesmaids and other attendants arrive at the church, followed by
your mother, the groom's parents and other members of
both families. The bridal party and the parents wait in the
vestibule while the other relatives are seated.

Five minutes before the ceremony, the mother of the groom is
escorted to her seat in the first pew on the right side of the
aisle. The father of the groom follows a few feet behind the
usher escorting his wife, then takes his seat beside her. You
and your father arrive in a chauffered limousine about this
time. If possible, park at a back entrance where you won't
be seen by late-arriving guests. Your mother is escorted to
her seat in the front pew. If guests are still waiting at this
time, however, they should be seated first. The bride's mother
is always the last person seated by an usher. As she starts
down the aisle, you and your father join the waiting members of the wedding party.

One minute before the ceremony, two ushers walk in step to the
front of the aisle to lay the aisle ribbons and canvas. The
ribbons, used only at very formal weddings, remind guests
to stay in their places until the parents and other relatives
have been escorted out. They are usually folded over the
second or third pew on each side so the ushers can just pick up
the ends, loop them over each pew, and fasten them at the

rear. White aisle canvas is sometimes used to protect the bride's dress and train, but is often omitted in a carpeted aisle, and may be dangerous if laid over smooth marble or stone. When used, it is folded accordian style in front of the altar steps until all guests have been seated. The ushers then pick up the outside edges and return up the aisle, pulling the runner smoothly behind them. (If they resist the temptation to turn around and check it, the canvas will be straight.) Once the ribbons and canvas are in place, the ushers return to the vestibule and take their places for the procession.

THE PROCESSION

The procession should begin as soon as possible after the time set for the ceremony.

In Protestant services, the congregation stands as soon as the wedding march begins, the clergyman enters and takes his place at the front of the church. The groom and best man follow him to a position just in front of the first, right-hand pew, and all turn to watch the procession.

The ushers enter from the back of the church in pairs, shortest first, followed by the bridesmaids. If there is an odd usher or bridesmaid, the shortest attendant leads off alone. The maid or matron of honor comes next, followed by the ring bearer, if there is one, and the flower girl(s). The pages, if any, follow the bride, carrying her train.

Catholic brides and grooms may follow the same procedure, or they may forgo the traditional procession and be met together by the priest at the church door.

Jewish processions vary according to local tradition, whether Orthodox, Conservative or Reform and according to the preference of the families. In the simplest Reform

PROCESSIONAL: 1) Bride, 2) Groom, 3) Maid of Honor, 4) Best Man, 5) Bridesmaids, 6) Ushers, 7) Flower Girl, 8) Ring bearer, 9) Father of the Bride, 10) Clergyman.

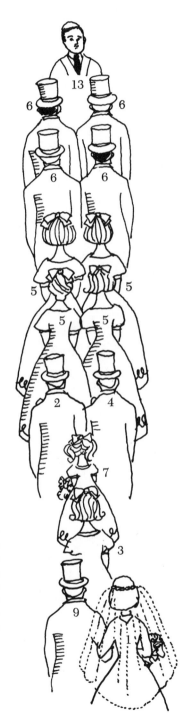

1. Bride, 2. Groom, 3. Maid of Honor, 4. Best Man, 5. Bridesmaids, 6. Ushers, 7. Flower Girl, 8. Ring bearer, 9. Father of the Bride, 10. Mother of the Bride, 11. Father of the Groom, 12. Mother of the Groom, 13. Clergyman.

service, the ushers lead the procession in pairs, followed by the bridesmaids in pairs. The groom comes down the aisle next, with his best man, followed by the maid of honor, the flower girl, if there is one, and the bride on her father's right. The groom's parents and the bride's mother may join in the procession and remain standing under the *chupa* or canopy during the service. The most elaborate procession may be led by the rabbi and cantor, followed by the couples' grandparents, the ushers, the bridesmaids, the best man, the groom and his parents, the bride's honor attendants, her flower girl(s), and the bride with her parents. Ask your rabbi how he prefers to organize the procession, and take into account the amount of space available for the wedding party to stand in.

In the Quaker service, there may be no procession and the bride and groom speak from their seats.

Civil ceremonies are usually quite small, with the bride preceded by one attendant, escorted into the room by her father and given over to the groom, who waits with the judge and the best man. In a large ceremony conducted by a judge or other official, you may choose any format of procession that is dignified and convenient.

ALTAR PROCEDURES

When the bridal party reaches the first row of seats, they form one of two alternate arrangements. In the first, the ushers all turn right to form a diagonal line behind the groom and the best man; the bridesmaids form a similar line on the left side, with each one turning in place to face the aisle. In the second plan, each pair of attendants separates at the front, with one going to each side. Thus, ushers and bridesmaids alternate in similar lines on both sides. They may stand side by side, or the bridesmaids may stand one step in front of the ushers. Children may stand through the ceremony, as shown on page 94, or be seated in the second or third pew with their parents.

In the Protestant service, as you reach the head of the aisle where your groom is waiting, you leave your father's arm and take one step forward. The groom steps forward and stands to your right. The maid of honor and best man take up positions on either side of the bride and groom while the other attendants turn to face the altar. Your father remains standing one step behind and to your left until the minister asks, "Who gives this woman to be married?"

In Catholic ceremonies and others in which the bride is not actually given away, however, your father turns and joins your mother in the first pew as soon as he has escorted you to the altar. In the Jewish ceremony, all the parents may remain standing throughout.

AT THE ALTAR: 1) Bride, 2) Groom, 3) Maid of Honor, 4) Best Man, 5) Bridesmaids, 6) Ushers, 7) Flower Girl, 8) Ring bearer, 9) Father of the Bride, 10) Clergyman.

JEWISH WEDDING: 1) Bride, 2) Groom, 3) Maid of Honor, 4) Best Man, 5) Bridesmaids, 6) Ushers, 7) Father of the Bride, 8) Mother of the Bride, 9) Father of the Groom, 10) Mother of the Groom, 11) Rabbi.

If you are required to kneel or climb steps during the ceremony, your groom usually takes your arm and helps you up and down. When the ceremony is over and the clergyman has congratulated the two of you, your face veil is lifted by the groom or the maid of honor. The traditional kiss may follow, or you may simply turn to face your guests. The maid of honor puts your bouquet in your right hand and arranges your train in preparation for the recessional.

THE RECESSIONAL

When the organist begins the recessional music, you'll take your groom's right arm and start up the aisle together. Your attendants — starting with the children — quickly fall into step behind you. Walking single file from their ceremony positions, they meet in the center and proceed up the aisle in pairs: the maid of honor on the right arm of the best man, each bridesmaid on the arm of an usher and extra ushers walking together at the end.

On reaching the vestibule, the designated ushers return to escort the mothers and honored guests from the church and to roll up the pew ribbons. The rest of the wedding party departs immediately in the waiting cars. At a very formal wedding, there may be a canopy and carpet to protect your dress as you and your groom dash from the church door to the car that takes you to the reception. Parking spaces are usually reserved for the cars of the bridal party so they can proceed to the reception without delay.

SPECIAL VARIATIONS

If your father has died, you may ask your brother, uncle, cousin or another close relative, a family friend or an usher to escort you down the aisle. Then your mother may give you away. In some ceremonies, she merely nods or says "I do," from her place in the first row at the appropriate time. When the bride's right hand is placed in the clergyman's hand, the best man usually escorts the bride's mother to her side.

If your parents are divorced, your father may still give you away. Instead of sitting down with your mother, however, he takes his place in the third row. If you prefer, your step-father or another male relative to whom you feel very close may walk you down the aisle. If divorced parents are included in the Jewish processional, only the parent and step-

6

5

6

5

6

5

6

5

4

3

8

7

1   2

RECESSIONAL: 1) Bride, 2) Groom, 3) Maid of Honor, 4) Best Man, 5) Bridesmaids, 6) Ushers, 7) Flower Girl, 8) Ring bearer.

parent with whom the bride or groom lives takes part. In this case the multiplicity of grandparents may be overwhelming and they may all, properly, be seated.

If a church has two center aisles, it's customary to use the left aisle for the procession, and the right aisle for the recessional. Sometimes the second aisle is closed off, and the ceremony proceeds as if there were only one aisle. When both aisles are used, the church is divided in half so that the bride's relatives and friends sit on both sides of the left aisle, the groom's on the right aisle. The two sets of parents sit in the center section: the bride's on the left half, the groom's on the right.

If you plan a receiving line immediately after the service, you and your attendants may start forming a line in the vestibule or on the steps as soon as you get to these posts. Your parents are the last to get into position and the first to greet guests as they leave. It's not necessary to receive wedding guests at this time unless there are a number of them who have not been invited to the reception.

SEMIFORMAL WEDDINGS

Most formal wedding procedures also apply to semiformal weddings. A smaller wedding party seldom includes children. There are usually fewer guests at a semiformal wedding, and pew ribbons, aisle carpets and canopies are usually omitted if you don't wear a long wedding dress and train. For details on semiformal home or garden weddings, see Chapter IX.

INFORMAL WEDDINGS

Guests at an informal wedding seat themselves as soon as they arrive. When it's time for the ceremony to begin, you and your groom, the maid of honor and the best man all take your appointed places in front of the clergyman. At the end of the short ceremony, without a recessional, you'll turn to greet your guests.

9
Special Weddings

THE MILITARY WEDDING

THE EXTRA FLOURISH and splendor of a military wedding appeal to many brides who marry commissioned officers on active duty. The outstanding characteristic of a military wedding is the traditional arch of sabers (swords in the Navy) under which the bride and groom walk at the end of the ceremony. This arch is formed by the ushers — all fellow officers of the groom in full dress uniform.

A groom in any branch of military service — whether he's an officer or not — may be married in uniform, but swords and sabers are carried only by officers in full dress uniform (blue in winter, white in summer). Like the men in any other wedding party, those in a military wedding should be dressed alike. One or two exceptions are sometimes made to allow your brothers to participate in the wedding, but your father is usually the only man in the procession in civilian clothes. Military decorations are worn by men in uniform instead of boutonnières. Swords and sabers are usually carried, rather than worn, so they don't get in the way when the ushers are seating guests.

Full dress military uniforms are formal attire, and are worn only if you wear a long wedding dress. The bridesmaids, mothers and wedding guests dress as they would for any other formal wedding at the same hour and season.

Most military weddings take place in military chapels — including those at West Point, Annapolis and the Air Force Academy — but other locations are acceptable. Decorations usually include an American flag and the standards of the groom's own military unit. Floral decorations are optional, but are often included for large weddings. Military rules on these and all other aspects of a military wedding should be verified with the proper authorities.

Invitations and announcements for a military wedding differ only in that the groom's rank and service are indicated. If your fiancé is a junior officer (below the rank of Army or Air Force Captain or Naval Commander), his title appears under his name, followed by the branch of service on the same line. The title of a senior officer precedes his name, and his branch is indicated on the following line, because "Mr." is never used to address or refer to an officer on active duty. (See Chapter V for additional details on the use of military titles.)

The procession for a military wedding follows standard procedures, but the recessional includes the traditional arch of steel. This may be formed outside the church, in front of the chancel, or both, depending on church rules, the branch of service and personal preference. The commands are usually issued by the head usher, starting with "Center face," the signal to form two facing lines. When the order "Arch sabers" (or "Draw swords") is given, each usher raises his saber in his right hand with the cutting edge on top. After you and your groom have passed under the arch, the sabers are sheathed or returned to the "carry" position. When the arch is formed inside, the bride and groom wait in the vestibule until the ushers are in place at the chapel door or on the steps.

The reception following a military wedding often features appropriate military decorations and music. These might include miniature flags and the theme song of the groom's branch of the service. At a sitdown reception, military guests, including the groom's commanding officer and immediate superiors, are seated by order of rank. The final military tradition is the use of the groom's saber or sword to cut the wedding cake.

THE DOUBLE WEDDING

Although any good friends or close relatives may have a double wedding, it's usually two sisters near to each other in age who choose to share their day. The main appeal of a double wedding is the saving — emotional as well as financial — it offers to families facing two successive weddings. A girl without such factors to consider is less inclined to share the spotlight on her wedding day.

Invitations to a double wedding are usually issued jointly as shown on page 57. If the brides are not sisters, however, separate invitations may be sent. It is customary for each couple in a double wedding to have their own attendants, but the two wedding parties are usually the same size. The brides often serve as each other's maid and matron of honor, but this is optional.

Double weddings are usually formal and follow the same rules of dress as any other formal wedding. Both sets of ushers dress exactly alike, while the bridesmaids wear dresses of the same length and formality. The styles and colors may be different so long as they harmonize. The brides usually wear different dresses, but their trains and veils should be about the same length.

When the two brides are sisters, the older usually takes precedence. Otherwise, the order of the ceremony and the seating arrangements must be worked out carefully in advance. If there are two aisles, the processions and recessionals may take place simultaneously, one on each side. When there is only one aisle, one set of parents must relinquish their right to the front row; or both sets may share this honor.

With a single aisle, the two grooms walk in together behind the clergyman and take their places side by side, each with his own best man behind him. The future husband of the older or first bride stands nearest the aisle. Both sets of ushers, paired by height, lead the procession. The bridesmaids, the maid of honor and the flower girl of the older bride come next, followed by the first bride on her father's arm. The second set of attendants and the younger bride follow in similar fashion. At a double wedding of sisters, a brother or other male relative may escort the second bride to the altar, but her father gives her away.

On reaching the head of the aisle, the attendants usually separate so that those of the older bride are all on the left, those of the younger on the right. The two couples stand side by side in front of the clergyman with the first bride on the left. In a double wedding of sisters, the father stands behind the older bride until he gives her away, then moves over to give his second daughter away before taking his seat. A joint ceremony is usually divided into segments, with the two couples completing each segment in turn. After the marriage vows are taken, the final blessing may be given to both couples at the same time.

At the close of the service, the two couples may kiss and turn simultaneously to face their guests. The recession is led by the older sister and her husband, followed by the younger couple. The two sets of honor attendants come next, followed by the bridesmaids and ushers in pairs. When each bride acts as the other's honor attendant, the best men escort bridesmaids in the recessional, with the extra ushers bringing up the rear.

A joint reception always follows a double wedding. When the brides are not sisters, each family forms a separate receiving line. Sisters receive in the same line with the older bride and her husband before the younger couple. To keep the line at a manageable length, the fathers seldom participate. If there is a large wedding party, including separate honor attendants, all the bridesmaids may also be excused from the receiving line. The size of the wedding party determines whether it's better to have a joint bridal table or separate ones.

THE HOME WEDDING

A home wedding may hold a sentimental attraction for you. Your own home or that of a relative or close friend can provide a unique setting for your wedding.

For a religious ceremony at home, a substitute altar and a kneeling bench or cushions may be necessary. These are set up in front of an attractive background — a fireplace or floral screen, for example. Formal seating is not needed, but chairs may be provided for guests. These are usually arranged in rows on either side of an "aisle." Ribbons or ropes of flowers and greens may also be used to form a pathway to the altar.

Guests at a home wedding are usually greeted by the bride's mother or a friend as they arrive. She may be assisted by the maid of honor (who is responsible, also, for meeting the officiating clergyman or judge and showing him where to change, if necessary). The groom's parents may mingle with the guests or wait with their son and the best man until they take their places for the ceremony. An usher or male relative usually escorts your mother to her place when the ceremony is about to begin. For a semiformal wedding at home, a modified procession, without ushers, is customary. When the signal is given, the clergyman, groom and best man walk to their places. The bridesmaids, if any, and the maid of honor make their entrance from an adjacent room or down a flight of stairs. Your father may meet you at the bottom of the stairs or at the entrance to the room where the ceremony will take place, then escort you to your groom's side.

At the end of a ceremony at home, your groom will kiss you immediately, to make sure that no one else breaks tradition by kissing you first. Without a recessional, you then turn to receive the good wishes of your relatives and friends. A formal receiving line is not necessary unless there are a great many guests. When you have spoken briefly to everyone, you may lead the way to the area where refreshments are served.

THE OUTDOOR WEDDING

A formal garden wedding is conducted much as is any home wedding. The "altar" is usually set up in front of the most scenic spot, such as a trellis, flowering hedge or summer-house. (A florist will create any of these for you.) If there is no garden path, you may indicate an aisle with rows of chairs, flowery standards or ropes of ribbon and greens. An aisle canvas is used when the bride wears a long dress. A standard procession is usually included, but the recessional is omitted. At the close of the ceremony, you and your groom turn to receive the greetings of your parents and attendants, then join them in forming a receiving line. Refreshments at a garden reception are usually served under shade trees or a tent. It's also wise to have a tent or some other form of protection available in case of bad weather.

A wedding at an outdoor site not near a private home requires special preparations. Be sure guests know how to get there; send a map with the invitations or after you receive acceptances if the words "Frontier Trail," for example, won't be enough to guide them. Be sure there is sufficient parking and turn-around space off the road. Otherwise, arrange for transportation — perhaps a school bus — from the nearest parking spot. Consult the State Highway Patrol for assistance. If you are not near a house and you expect the celebration to go on more than an hour, you will have to arrange access to rest rooms for the guests. And if possible, try to be near cover where the whole assembly can move in case of rain.

THE SECOND MARRIAGE

A second-time bride may be married in a formal, religious ceremony if her faith permits, but older widows and divorcées often choose simple ceremonies attended only by relatives and a few close friends. A second-time bride never wears stark white or a veil, traditional symbols of chastity; otherwise she follows the usual rules of dress for the degree of formality she chooses.

A second marriage may do without a procession, for the bride is not given away. Attendants may be limited to a maid or matron of honor and a best man, but there may be bridesmaids and as many ushers as are needed to seat the guests. The children of a first marriage may participate in their parents' second weddings· if they are old enough to understand the circumstances and are happy about the wedding.

The bride removes the engagement and wedding rings given her by her first husband when she announces her engagement. If her new husband has no objections, she may continue to wear her first engagement ring on her right hand.

The size of the guest list determines what invitations are correct for a second marriage. Handwritten invitations are suitable for a small ceremony, but engraved invitations may be sent for a large reception. Formal announcements are also proper for a second marriage.

A prior marriage of the groom has far less effect upon the size and style of the wedding. A formal church ceremony is proper if it doesn't violate any religious rule.

THE OLDER BRIDE

A mature woman usually does not choose an elaborate train and veil designed for a girl of twenty. She may wear a long white dress if she wishes, but it should be simple and appropriate for her age. A mature bride may have a church wedding with two or three attendants, but she should not ask her own contemporaries to wear youthful bridesmaids' dresses. Junior bridesmaids or flower girls make charming attendants for an older bride. Whether or not she is given away, she may be escorted down the aisle in the standard procession.

A large and festive reception is always in order — no matter how old the bride and groom may be. Mature couples, however, often omit such frivolous touches as throwing the bouquet and garter.

THE CLERGYMAN'S WEDDING

Like any other groom, a clergyman is married in the bride's church or synagogue by her own minister or rabbi. If you are a parishioner of your groom's, his superior or another clergyman of equal rank may perform the ceremony. A clergyman may be married in his clerical garb, in formal attire with a clerical collar or in regular dress. The formality of the wedding and the customs of his denomination are determining factors.

If your father is a clergyman, he may officiate at the ceremony. Your brother, uncle or another male relative may escort you down the aisle, then take his seat. Your mother may step forward at the proper time in the ceremony to give you away.

THE CIVIL CEREMONY

Most civil ceremonies are performed in a courthouse, a judge's chambers or the home of a justice of the peace. These are small, simple ceremonies which follow the rules for an informal wedding. A small reception may follow such a ceremony.

Under certain circumstances a large formal wedding may be performed by a judge or other civil authority. These weddings may take place at home or in a club or ballroom, and be followed by large receptions. An aisle is formed between rows of chairs, and the usual procedures for a formal wedding are followed.

10
Rules and Rituals

AMERICAN MARRIAGE CEREMONIES — whether Protestant, Catholic, Jewish or nonsectarian — have many similarities, but the differences are significant. It's important, therefore, for every member of the wedding party to be familiar with the basic rules and rituals of the faith in which the ceremony is performed. And, particularly if you hope to plan a ceremony outside the traditional format of the church, it is important to know the legal requirements of the state issuing the marriage certificate. In all cases, the officiating clergyman or civil officer should always be consulted about specific details, as, even within a given faith, traditions vary.

PROTESTANT WEDDINGS

Almost all Protestant churches use the standard wedding service, and most require the congregation to remain standing during part of the ceremony. Although there are no laws prohibiting marriage on any day of the year, many Protestant clergymen are reluctant to perform wedding ceremonies on Sundays and other religious holidays. Rules on music vary, but prior approval of a church authority is usually required. There are no fixed rules on attire, but bare dresses look wrong in any church. The following variations affect Protestant marriages.

EPISCOPAL: The Episcopal church usually frowns on formal weddings during Lent. The remarriage of divorced persons is seldom allowed, but dispensations are sometimes granted. The baptism of at least one party to the marriage is usually required for a church wedding. A Nuptial Mass similar to the Catholic ceremony may follow a wedding in the "high" or Anglo-Catholic branch of the Episcopal church. Head coverings are usually required for women in an Episcopal church.

QUAKER: A Quaker wedding requires prior approval (which may take up to three months) from the monthly meeting of the Society of Friends. The marriage itself takes place during a meeting for worship where those in attendance, including all members of the meeting, meditate quietly. The bridal couple may enter the meeting together or in the usual procession; but the bride is not given away. On reaching the head of the aisle, the bridal party sits down on benches facing the meeting. After the traditional Quaker silence, the bride and groom rise, join hands and say their vows to each other. The groom speaks his promises first, then the bride. No third person pronounces them man and wife because Friends believe that God alone can create such a union.

After the bride and groom complete their vows and take their seats, the marriage certificate is brought for them to sign — the bride using her new married name for the first time. The certificate is then read aloud by a person designated in advance. The meeting continues while those assembled share in the worship through prayer or spoken messages. When the meeting has a pastor, he naturally takes part in the wedding. When they sense that the meeting should close, the bride and groom shake hands and leave the room. All guests sign the marriage certificate before leaving.

Neither a bridal party nor an exchange of rings is necessary at a Quaker wedding, but both are customary today. The use of music and floral decorations is left up to the individual couple, but the traditional Quaker wedding is a very simple ceremony.

CHRISTIAN SCIENCE: Readers of the Christian Science faith are not ordained and may not perform marriages. When members of the faith marry, the ceremony may be performed by any ordained minister or proper legal authority.

MORMON: The Church of Jesus Christ of Latter Day Saints has two kinds of marriage. The first is for the faithful deemed fit for marriage in the temples of the church by members of the Holy Priesthood. Such a couple are wed "for time and all eternity" instead of "until death you do part," and their children are believed to belong to them for all eternity as well. Mormons who are not considered worthy of marriage

in a temple are wed in civil ceremonies performed by bishops
of the church or other legal authorities.

ROMAN CATHOLIC WEDDINGS

While Catholic marriages are performed and Nuptial
Masses celebrated during Lent and Advent, the decoration
and style may be somewhat restricted.

When both the bride and the groom are Catholic, the
banns (announcements) of marriage are published in the
parish churches of both at the principal Masses on three
consecutive Sundays or Holy Days before the wedding. The
banns are not usually published for a mixed marriage, but
the required dispensation from the bishop of the diocese is
now easily received. The nonCatholic party to a mixed marriage need not be baptized, but must be free to marry in the
Catholic church. The marriage of divorced persons is not
allowed in the Catholic church unless the previous marriage
has been declared null by a church court.

A Catholic bride must have the permission of her own
pastor to be married in another parish. The officiating priest
will require proof of Baptism for baptized persons and
evidence of freedom to marry. Catholic weddings are rarely
performed outside of a church, although mixed marriages
are sometimes performed in the church of the nonCatholic.
In such cases a Roman Catholic priest may officiate with the
nonCatholic minister pronouncing a prayer or blessing over
the couple.

The procession in a Catholic wedding may follow the
procedures for a Protestant ceremony, except that the bride
is not given away. Some couples are choosing to be greeted

by the priest at the vestibule door. After the greeting, the priest leads the procession to the altar. Variations of these two plans, or combinations of them are also accepted. The traditional wedding marches are not allowed in many Catholic dioceses, for they are secular music. See Chapter XII for suggested alternatives and consult the officiating priest. It's customary for the maid of honor and the best man to be practicing Catholics. Head coverings are required for all women at a Catholic wedding, guests as well as the wedding party.

A Nuptial Mass may be arranged for almost any Catholic wedding. In the Nuptial Mass for a mixed marriage, however, nonCatholics do not take communion. The brief wedding ceremony is incorporated in the Mass, which may last as long as an hour.

The bride and groom and their honor attendants usually enter the sanctuary, and the rest of the wedding party may follow if there is space. These details are usually worked out with the priest at the rehearsal.

Catholic members of the wedding party usually receive Holy Communion. Special Mass books — which may be imprinted with the names of the bridal couple and the date of the ceremony — are often distributed to guests so they may follow the ritual of the Mass. Although nonCatholic guests needn't give the responses, they may kneel and stand at the proper times in the ceremony.

EASTERN ORTHODOX WEDDINGS

The churches of the Eastern Rite — including Greek and Russian Orthodox — are similar in many ways to the Roman

Catholic, but they do not recognize the authority of the Pope in Rome. Mixed marriages are allowed, but the non-Orthodox party to the marriage must be a baptized Christian. Eastern Rite churches permit the remarriage of those who've received religious decrees of divorce or annulment. The banns of marriage may be proclaimed, but are not necessary.

Marriages may not be solemnized in an Orthodox church during any season of fasting, or on the eve of certain holy days, during the week after Easter or in the two weeks after Christmas. Orthodox weddings usually take place in the afternoon or early evening. They seldom include a Mass; the marriage itself is a long ceremony full of symbolism and pageantry. Traditionally, the only music allowed in an Orthodox church is that of an unaccompanied choir, and the ancient Byzantine and Russian chants prevail, but organs are now used in some Greek churches in America.

The standard wedding procession in which the bride's father gives her away is customary in an Eastern Rite church. The size of the wedding party and its arrangement during the ceremony are matters of personal taste and local custom. The maid of honor and the best man (called *koumbari* in the Greek Church), however, usually have more complex duties in an Orthodox wedding. A face veil must be worn by a Greek bride, but is optional in the Russian church. The guests at a Russian Orthodox wedding usually remain standing throughout the ceremony, but in Greek churches in America, they are often allowed to sit during the less sacred parts of the service.

An Orthodox wedding begins with a betrothal ritual, usually at the front or center of the church. This includes the blessing and exchange of rings which are customarily worn by both bride and groom on their right hands. The rings are exchanged between the bride and groom three times, signifying the Holy Trinity.

At the close of the betrothal part of the service, the bride and groom usually move up the center aisle of the church to positions before a stand in front of the *ikonostasis* or altar screen. Their hands are linked by the priest, who sings "The Hand of God Descends." Two crowns (often replaced by wreaths of green foliage or waxy flowers and ribbons) are placed on the heads of the bride and groom and exchanged three times. This exchange is sometimes made by the *koumbari* holding the crowns above the heads of the bridal couple. After the Gospel is read, a cup of wine is shared three times by the bride and groom to signify the cups of joy and sorrow they will share. Afterwards, the wine is also shared by the *koumbari*. The bride and groom are then led around the ceremonial table or lecturn three times with their right hands bound together.

After the recessional in a Greek church, friends of the family often stand on the church steps and distribute festive packages of sugar-coated almonds to the guests. This has the same significance as the shower of rice traditional at other weddings.

JEWISH WEDDINGS

No single set of rules applies to all Jewish weddings, for there are significant differences between the Orthodox, Conservative and Reform branches of the faith. Individual rabbis and synagogues also have their own variations. It is important, therefore, to verify all rules and procedures with your own rabbi before making definite plans.

Orthodox and Conservative rabbis do not perform mixed marriages, and do not recognize any divorces except those granted by a religious decree. Most Reform rabbis, on the other hand, recognize civil divorce, and some perform mixed marriages. Jewish weddings may take place at any time except on the Sabbath (from sundown on Friday until sundown on Saturday), on holy days, during a three week period in midsummer and during most of Passover and Shavuoth. Most are performed on Saturday evening after sundown or on Sunday.

A Jewish wedding may be held in almost any location, so many do not take place in synagogues. It is more usual in some areas for the ceremony to be performed at a club, hotel or catering hall where the traditional wedding feast and dancing follow. Conventional wedding attire — including a face veil for the bride — is usually worn. In an Orthodox wedding, all the men must have their heads covered by skull caps (*yarmulkes*) or silk top hats.

At many Jewish weddings, the bride and her attendants receive the guests before the ceremony in an anteroom of the wedding hall. The bride's family may then be seated on the right side of the hall or temple and the groom's family on the left, before any of the other guests are seated.

The order of this procession and the positions during the ceremony are set by custom. Orthodox and Conservative processions, however, usually include the groom and both sets of parents. (See page 91.) The ushers walk down the aisle first, followed by the bridesmaids and the ringbearer. Sometimes the ushers and maids form a guard of honor for the rest of the procession to walk through.

Jewish marriages are traditionally performed under a *chupa*, a richly ornamented canopy symbolizing the sky and supported by decorated standards. It is usually placed in front of an attractive background at one end of the room or in front of the ark in a temple. The procession walks toward the canopy, with each person taking a prescribed position

under or near it. The bride stands on the groom's right under
the canopy, and the rabbi stands facing them. It's also customary for the honor attendants to stand under the *chupa* —
the maid of honor on the bride's right, the best man on the
groom's left. When space permits, the parents sometimes
stand alongside or directly behind their children under the
canopy. The bridesmaids and ushers usually stand in single
file on either side of the *chupa* as shown in the illustration on
page 93.

For the marriage ceremony, Orthodox and Conservative
rabbis usually stand next to a small table covered in white
and set with two cups of ritual wine and a glass wrapped in a
piece of white silk or a napkin. The service begins with the
blessing of the wine. The rabbi then hands the wine to the
groom who sips it and passes it to his bride. The groom
places a plain gold wedding band on the bride's right index
finger and recites the proper responses. (The bride may move
the ring to her third finger later.) After a short address by the
rabbi, the traditional Seven Blessings are given, followed by
the ceremonial drinking of the second cup of wine. The final
ritual is the crushing of the wrapped wine glass on the floor
beneath the groom's heel.

The order of the recessional varies, but it's always led by
the bride and groom. They are usually followed by the
bride's parents, the groom's parents, the maid of honor on
the best man's arm, then the rabbi, with pairs of bridesmaids
and ushers bringing up the rear.

In a Reform wedding the procession, recessional and other
ceremonial details may follow the procedures used in the
Protestant service. The traditional wedding marches are
often used, and the bride's ring is placed on her left hand.
The marriage may or may not be performed under a *chupa*.

The wedding feast is traditionally important to a Jewish
wedding. Frequently more lavish than a Christian reception,

it always includes a marriage grace. The receiving line and other details are similar to other wedding receptions.

VARIATIONS

Almost all religions allow certain variations in their services. You and your fiancé should talk together about what you want your ceremony to express. Review the standard vows — is this what you want to announce to your assembled friends and family? If there is more, and it can be celebrated with dignity, changes in your wedding service can greatly enrich the meaning of this day in your memory. Some of the classic additions to the wedding service are included in Chapter XII.

Naturally, if religion is an important part of your background, you will want to marry within the requirements of your faith. If, however, yours is to be a free-form celebration that does not lend itself to shaping around the basic religious or legal requirements, you may wish to separate your wedding from your official marriage, which can be performed neatly, swiftly and legally at city hall a day earlier or later.

11
Your Reception

SETTING THE STYLE

AS LONG AS it affords your relatives and friends an opportunity to greet you, wish you well and help you celebrate
the happy occasion, a wedding reception may be anything
from a few friends sharing a homemade wedding cake to a
gala banquet with an orchestra for dancing. It may be held
in your home or garden, at a private club or church hall, in
a large restaurant or ballroom. You may serve punch and
wedding cake, cocktails and hors d'oeuvres or imported
champagne and a five-course dinner. If you're being married
early in the day, your reception may also take the form of a
breakfast, a luncheon or a tea.

You may choose to have a simple reception — wedding

cake and a beverage to toast with is all you really need — in order to invite all the ceremony guests on to the reception.

THE RECEIVING LINE

Guests should be able to move down the line, past the bride's book, if there is one, and into the area where the refreshments are served. At a large reception, you may serve champagne or provide ice water or iced tea for guests as they wait. In any case, be sure that the line is placed far enough from the entrance that waiting guests do not spill out into the corridor or parking lot.

Your mother is the first to greet the guests. Your groom's mother stands next to her, followed by his father. You are next in line, on your husband's right if possible, with the

THE RECEIVING LINE: 1) Bride, 2) Groom, 3) Maid of Honor, 4) Bridesmaids, 5) Mother of the Bride, 6) Mother of the Groom, 7) Father of the Groom.

maid of honor or one of your bridesmaids on his left (they may take turns filling this position if you like). Your father may also join the line and stand between the two mothers, but participation by both fathers is optional. The bride's father usually circulates, and the groom's father may do the same. The best man, ushers, and child attendants usually do not participate in the receiving line.

If you have no mother or stepmother to receive guests, your father may stand at the head of the line with your aunt, grandmother or sister. If most of the guests know her, she may stand in front of your father. When the reception is given by persons other than the bride's parents, the host and hostess are the first in line to receive guests.

You may choose to hold your bouquet in the receiving line or put it aside, but the bridesmaids always hold their flowers in their left hands. All the women may wear their hats and gloves in the line, but the men must remove theirs. Guests going along a receiving line are introduced to each person in turn, starting with your mother. If necessary they start by introducing themselves. Although you precede your groom in line, he should reach out to introduce his own relatives and friends. After the last guest has been welcomed, the two of you should move to cut the cake or start the dancing.

SEATING ARRANGEMENTS

Even when the guests serve themselves from a buffet, the bridal party is usually served at their own table. The table, which may be any shape, is usually covered with a white lace or damask cloth reaching to the floor. It may be decorated with garlands of greens, candles and low bouquets —

anything that doesn't obscure the bridal party. Unless the table is round, seating is usually on one side only. You and your groom sit together at the head or center of the table, with the groom at your left and ushers and bridesmaids in alternating seats on each side. (See sketch below.)

Members of the wedding party are always seated at the bride's table, and when the party is small, the husbands and wives of married attendants, the parents and the clergyman may join them. In most cases, however, there is a separate parents' table. This is usually a rectangular table with your mother and father in the places of honor at opposite ends. The groom's father sits on your mother's right while the clergyman sits on her left. The groom's mother is seated on your father's right, with the clergyman's wife (or his assistant) on his left. At the reception following a Jewish wedding, the parents and grandparents of the bride and groom, the rabbi, the cantor, and their wives may be seated at the bridal table, and the bridesmaids and ushers seated among the other guests. Or you may arrange two parents' tables, one

THE BRIDE'S TABLE: 1) Bride, 2) Groom, 3) Maid of Honor, 4) Best Man, 5) Bridesmaids, 6) Ushers.

for your parents and one for the groom's, so that more friends and relatives may be among those honored by a seat at the parents' tables.

White cards mark each place at the bride's and parents' tables, but are optional elsewhere. Guests may find their own seats with special friends and relatives, or you may do a complete seating plan and mark each place. In this case you may want to mix your family and your groom's and seat guests with others you think they'll like, just as you would for any party. If you so seat a great many guests, you may want to have table numbers, and a card placed in an envelope on a table near the entrance to tell each guest where to sit. The seating of guests is not necessary, of course, at tea, cocktail and buffet receptions.

REFRESHMENTS

A wedding reception always includes wedding cake and a beverage suitable for drinking a toast, but nothing more is required. Anything else you serve depends on your budget, local custom and the time of day. Champagne is traditional and appropriate at any hour. It may be served during the entire reception or only for toasts. Champagne punch and mixed drinks are also popular in some areas. Tea receptions are sometimes completely dry, but may also include a choice of alcoholic and nonalcoholic punch. Ginger ale or white grape juice may be substituted for champagne, but coffee, tea and water are not used for toasts.

All daytime wedding receptions once were called breakfasts, but the term is rarely used today. After a morning wedding, however, you may still serve breakfast — fresh fruit, shirred eggs, country sausage, blueberry muffins and coffee, perhaps. Light luncheon fare is also appropriate. For example, the menu might include creamed chicken in pastry shells, buttered peas, a molded salad, hot biscuits and ice cream. A more substantial seated luncheon or buffet is often served after a high noon wedding.

Weddings starting between one and four in the afternoon are usually followed by tea or cocktail receptions. At a tea, you might serve sandwiches, nuts and mints. A cocktail reception might include a cold buffet or hot hors d'oeuvres, such as cocktail sausages, stuffed mushrooms and cheese puffs. A hot buffet or a seated dinner of at least three courses is commonly served following an evening wedding. After a late afternoon wedding, tea or cocktail fare may be sufficient. Your caterer or banquet manager can advise you on the most suitable dishes as well as on the quantities needed.

YOUR WEDDING CAKE

The wedding cake, in one form or another, has been an important part of wedding tradition since Roman days. Even if your wedding is attended only by the two witnesses and your parents, it's customary to celebrate with a wedding cake. This might be the traditional bride's cake, a groom's cake or a combination of the two.

The bride's cake is the familiar frothy white confection topped with flowers, wedding bells or similar ornaments. It usually includes several layers or tiers of light pound, sponge or lady cake. It's customary to cut the bride's cake and serve it at the reception, with extra slices provided for guests to take home. Tradition says that a piece of wedding cake under a girl's pillow will lead her to dream of her future husband. Napkins or tiny boxes may be supplied to those who want to take pieces of cake with them.

The less familiar groom's cake is a dark, rich fruit cake. You may have it packed in individual boxes to distribute to guests or save it to eat on your anniversaries. (The best way to do this is to have it sealed with brandy in a tin.) You may have it covered with icing and used as the top layer of the bride's cake.

The cake is usually given the spotlight on a table covered with a fine white cloth and trimmed with flowers.

You'll cut the wedding cake just before dessert at a luncheon or dinner reception, or just after the guests have been received at a tea or cocktail reception. Your groom places his right hand over yours and together you cut into the bottom layer with a ribbon-tied silver knife. The first slice is always shared by the bride and groom as a symbol of their willingness to share each other's lives from then on. The cake is then cut and served to the guests.

DANCING

Although not required, dancing adds a happy and festive note to any wedding reception. You don't have to have an orchestra to have dancing; a string trio, a piano or even a phonograph will do. (See Chapter XII.) At a hotel or club reception, the area in front of the bride's table is usually cleared for dancing. If you're having your reception at home, you might set aside one whole room for dancing. At a garden reception, guests may dance on the terrace or on a temporary wooden dance floor set up under a tent or over a pool.

The traditional "first dance" is your first as bride and groom. But there's no reason why your guests shouldn't begin dancing as soon as they have cleared the receiving line and the music starts playing. After you've caught your breath from greeting the guests, there is a pause in the music — or the strains of "Here Comes the Bride" — the floor clears, and dancing resumes with you and your groom circling the floor alone. You are next claimed by your father while your groom dances with his new mother-in-law. The best man and the father of the groom are your next two partners, while your husband takes your maid of honor and his own mother around the floor. The order of these traditional dances is optional, but they are usually completed before the guests join in again. You'll probably dance with each usher and your groom with each bridesmaid before the dancing ends. It's also customary for each man in the wedding party to request a dance with each bridesmaid and both mothers.

TOASTS

Toasts to the happy couple are a traditional part of wedding receptions. They may begin any time after the receiving line has ended and everyone has been served a glass of champagne or another suitable beverage. The first toast is always proposed by the best man. He may word it any way he likes, but a simple, heartfelt wish is more effective than a clever toast taken from a book. For example, he may merely say, "Here's to the bride and groom — may they always be as happy as they are today!" A longer toast might include personal references to the newlyweds. When the best man completes his toast, everyone (except you and your groom, of course) rises and drinks to it.

The groom usually respond by thanking his best man and offering a toast or two of his own — to you, to his parents or to his new in-laws. The ushers and fathers may then propose additional toasts if they wish. All those present — except the person being toasted — should raise their glasses to each toast. At the end of the toasts, the best man may, if you wish, read aloud any congratulatory telegrams sent by absent friends and relatives.

THROWING THE BOUQUET AND GARTER

Just before you change into your going-away clothes, word is passed to the bridesmaids and other single girls to gather at the bottom of a stairway, under a balcony or at some other convenient spot. If your going-away flowers are part of your bridal bouquet, remove them first. If you carry a prayerbook instead of a bouquet, you may throw the floral and ribbon streamers. Some brides turn and toss the bouquet over a shoulder, but if you'd like to aim at your sister or dear friend, you'll probably face the group as you throw. Tradition says that the girl who catches the bouquet will be the next bride.

The bride's garter (usually blue satin) may be thrown to the ushers and other bachelors. The groom removes it from your leg and you toss it, as you tossed the bouquet, with the man who catches it destined to be the next to marry.

12
Wedding Music

MUSIC CAN HELP create the mood of solemnity and joy you want in your marriage ceremony and can add a festive feeling to a wedding reception.

The rules on wedding music vary according to the religious faith and the individual clergyman. Some churches forbid or discourage secular music or require that all music be in praise of or a prayer to God. Others allow secular music to be played, but not sung.

Even if you are permitted to use the "Bridal Chorus" from *Lohengrin* ("Here Comes the Bride") or the "Wedding March" from Mendelssohn's *Midsummer Night's Dream*, you should explore the wealth of beautiful music that will be more truly your own. Consult the organist or choir director, buy and listen to records until you find just the piece you want.

MUSIC FOR PROTESTANT WEDDINGS

At a formal church wedding, it's customary to have a recital of organ music starting about thirty minutes before the ceremony. This music is usually played softly, but should not be monotonous in mood or tone. Among the many suitable pieces you might want to consider are "Sheep May Safely Graze," and "Sleepers Awake" by Bach; "Adagio in E from Violin Sonata" and "Air" by Handel; "Prelude number 2" by Mendelssohn and "My Jesus Calls to Me" by Brahms.

A choir may lead the procession, or you may have a vocal solo. Unless you know a truly skilled singer, it is best to omit this touch. Clergymen vary in their policies toward vocal music, and unless it is very important to you and your groom, you may well choose to follow the popular trend away from singing.

Procession music should be joyous and triumphal, but it needn't be in march tempo since the wedding party walks at a natural pace. A number of hymns have organ arrangements which meet the requirements beautifully. Among the most widely recommended selections for processions are Purcell's "Voluntary" and "Trumpet Tunes." Other good choices are Franck's "Fantasie in C," Brahms' "St. Anthony Chorale" from "Variations on a Theme by Haydn" and Telemann's "Heldenmusik."

Many of the pieces suggested for the wedding procession are suitable for the recessional as well. Selections from Handel and Purcell and Marcello's "Psalm 19" are also excellent. Your organist will be able to suggest many others.

MUSIC FOR CATHOLIC WEDDINGS

Secular music of all kinds — including the usual wedding marches — is prohibited in most Catholic churches. Liturgical music and the hymns sung at regular Masses are the general rule. A choir sometimes sings, but this is entirely optional and soloists are more often used. Solos are usually permitted at appropriate times before and during the ceremony. In addition to the permitted versions of the "Ave Maria," you might want the traditional "Panis Angelicus" by Franck or Mozart's "Ave Verum." It is now customary with the Mass in the vernacular to choose hymns which allow the congregation to participate. Folk music, if it is well performed, may also be acceptable. The procession and recessional pieces recommended for Protestant weddings are also generally accepted.

MUSIC FOR JEWISH WEDDINGS

Although instrumental music has been an essential part of Jewish weddings for centuries, there was never any music specifically created for this purpose. Contemporary Jewish musicians have attempted to fill this void, but their compositions have not gained full acceptance and popularity as yet. The wedding marches are permitted at many reform weddings, but Orthodox and Conservative rabbis generally frown upon their use.

READINGS FOR WEDDINGS

Any prayer, poem or other material you add to your wedding service should, of course, have special meaning to you. You might look for inspiration to Thoreau, the Song of Solomon in the Bible or to *The Prophet* by Kahlil Gibran.

MUSIC FOR WEDDING RECEPTIONS

Whether you plan to have dancing or not, you'll probably want to have some kind of music at your wedding reception — even if it's only from a phonograph. You may have a pianist playing in the background, a string trio in the corner, or a small orchestra on a raised platform. You may also want to have a soloist to sing some of your favorite songs.

Almost any popular songs or old standards are appropriate at a wedding reception. It's advisable to give the musicians a list of your favorites in advance. If you're fond of "Here Comes the Bride," have them play it as you and your groom enter the room. If there are songs you don't want played, specify these as well. Ordinarily the band leader can provide you with a list from which you can eliminate any that rankle. Be sure to specify what, if anything, you want played while you cut the cake, and as you leave. Otherwise the musicians may play "The Bride Cuts the Cake" to the tune of "The Farmer in the Dell" and "Toot-Toot-Tootsie Goodbye" whether you want these or not.

13
Wedding Flowers

FLOWERS HAVE BEEN a part of weddings for centuries. They are treasured for the beauty, color and wealth of tradition which they bring to marriage ceremonies of every size and description. Worn or carried by every member of the wedding party, flowers provide a decorative background for religious rites and reception festivities alike. A few well-placed flowers make the most austere church or chapel look festive and pretty and add an aura of romance to the most modest house or restaurant.

It's important to consult your florist in the early stages of your planning. He can advise you on the most appropriate flowers for various uses, and tell you which ones will be most readily available at the time of your wedding. He can show you samples of the various types and shapes of bouquets and of any blossoms with which you're unfamiliar. He might also suggest some attractive arrangements and color schemes to supplement your own ideas. You can have any flower you like — even out of season — for a price, because of hothouse growing and air shipping, but certain flowers become identified with the seasons in which they naturally bloom.

WEDDING BOUQUETS

A bouquet of flowers is traditionally carried by the bride and each of her attendants at all but the most informal weddings. It may be anything from a large armload of flowers to a small nosegay, but it should be scaled to your size and complement your dress. A loose cascade of feathered chrysanthemums, for example, might be stunning for a tall bride in a long flowing dress, but overpowering to a short girl with a simpler look.

Your bouquet may be made of any flowers in any colors you choose, though it is best to choose the natural hues of the flowers (that is, violets instead of purple-dyed carnations). Or you may choose all white, traditionally mixed with ivy, a symbol of fidelity, and other greens. White roses, orchids, carnations, stephanotis, lilies of the valley and gardenias are the favorite bridal flowers, but many others are used in season. Easter lilies, for example, make lovely spring bouquets, while summer arrangements often include delicate babies' breath or Queen Anne's lace.

Be sure to give your florist a complete description of your dress — including the silhouette, length, neckline and sleeves — so he can recommend an appropriate style for your bouquet. Cresent cascades, fan-shaped arrangements and colonial bouquets are all suitable for a bride to carry, but they don't look equally pretty with every dress.

The bridesmaids and the maid of honor usually carry similar arrangements of the same flowers, but the honor attendant often has a different shade or a contrasting color in her bouquet. It isn't necessary for your attendants' bouquets to be duplicates of your own, but they should have the same general feeling. If you plan to carry daisies, for example, your bridesmaids might carry daffodils or cornflowers, but not orchids. Various colors of roses and carnations are popular for bridesmaids' bouquets the year around, but some of the most attractive arrangements feature seasonal flowers. In spring, for example, your bridesmaids might wear pink dresses and carry dogwood, lilacs or anemones. Yellow daffodils and forsythia are also pretty with light blue or lavender dresses. Bridesmaids in a summer wedding might wear pale pink and carry red and white peonies, multicolored sweetpeas or pink and red larkspur. For a fall wedding, you might consider forest green dresses for your bridesmaids and russet colored chrysanthemums mixed with autumn leaves or sheaves of wheat for their bouquets. If you plan to be married in December, you might plan a red and white color scheme using poinsettias, roses or holly. Whatever you choose, be sure to give your florist a complete description of your bridesmaids' dresses and a swatch of fabric to guide him in designing appropriate bouquets.

Flower girls have traditionally carried baskets of loose petals to be strewn in the bride's path, but the danger of slipping on the petals has prompted some authorities to prohibit the practice. Thus, today's flower girl often carries a miniature bouquet of flowers arranged in a basket, attached to a muff or fashioned into a nosegay. Rosebuds, violets, lilies of the valley or other small blossoms are lovely.

FLOWERS TO WEAR

The bride at an informal wedding usually pins on her flowers instead of carrying a wedding bouquet. White orchids are popular with many brides, but you may wear any flowers you like as long as they complement your outfit. You might even choose a muff woven of greens and daisies. If you have a formal wedding, the orchid or other flowers from the center of your bouquet can be removed to wear on your going away costume if you like, or you may have the florist make up a fresh arrangement — perhaps in another color — to wear as you leave.

The mothers and grandmothers of the bride and groom are customarily presented with flowers to wear at the wedding. These may be made of any flowers that harmonize with their dresses, but personal preferences should be taken into consideration. Some women, for example, like nothing better than roses, but a mother with a rose garden in her back yard might prefer a cluster of cymbidium orchids.

PRAYER BOOK FLOWERS

In a formal or semiformal wedding, you may carry a flower-covered prayer book instead of a bouquet. This may be a new book purchased for the occasion or an old family Bible or missal. Whether new or old, the book may be covered in white silk or satin to harmonize with your dress. Although white orchids are favored for bridal prayer books, you may choose other flowers if you wish. A cascade of small blossoms or ribbon streamers intertwined with stephanotis or lilies of the valley is usually attached to the prayer book when the bride wears a long dress.

FLORAL HEADPIECES

Although silk flowers are much more common these days, headpieces made of real orange blossoms or other light flowers are still worn by some brides and bridesmaids. These are usually made in the form of a crescent that fits across the top of the head, or in a circle that sits on the crown. Such headpieces may be attached to a small comb or held in place with hairpins. A veil is usually attached to a bride's headpiece, but those worn by attendants often take the place of hats or veils.

BOUTONNIÈRES

It's traditional for the groom and every man in the wedding party — including the best man, the ushers and the fathers — to wear a boutonnière on his left lapel. White carnations are commonly worn by everyone except the groom and his best man. Your groom's boutonnière may follow tradition and be taken from your bouquet: a white rose, a sprig of stephanotis or a few lilies of the valley. The best man's boutonnière may match the groom's or it may be slightly different.

FLORAL DECORATIONS

Ceremony flowers vary considerably with the location and the size and style of the ceremony. In general, elaborate floral decorations are reserved for very large, formal weddings, but a plain chapel sometimes needs more decorations than an ornate cathedral. It's important to discuss your plans in advance with the proper authorities as well as with your florists, for some rules limit the color or placement of flowers for religious ceremonies.

Regardless of the size and style of your wedding, you'll want to have at least one vase of flowers on each side of the altar. You may also have a number of other arrangements. Many brides like to attach small sprays of flowers instead of the usual ribbon bows to the aisle posts. These may be placed on every second or third pew, or just on those reserved for relatives and special guests. If you're being married in a simple church with plain windows, you might want to put a festive arrangement of flowers and candles in each window sill. When guests are not expected to fill the space, it's nice to have a bank of ferns, palms or potted flowers to mark the section needed for the ceremony. Ropes of flowers interspersed with ivy or smilax might also be draped along the altar rail or used to partition the church.

You may choose any flowers you like. Altar arrangements are frequently made of the same flowers carried by the bridesmaids. Blossoms that are too fragile for bouquets also make marvelous ceremony decorations. In spring, for example, you might have pots of tulips, amaryllis, azaleas, geraniums or crocuses. Garlands of wisteria are nice for summer weddings, and potted rhododendron provides a pretty accent of color in winter.

Even the most attractive home or club needs assorted greens and flowers to form a simple aisle and a decorative background for the ceremony. Banks of ferns, baskets of cut flowers, or rows of potted plants may be used to partition the room into the appropriate sections. You might place a screen of greens and flowers behind the altar or kneeling bench and drape ropes of ribbon intertwined with tiny blossoms to indicate an aisle.

Reception flowers may be as simple or as elaborate as you wish. You may carry out your wedding color scheme by repeating the flowers in your bridesmaids' bouquets, or you may select something different to harmonize with the surroundings. It's customary to have floral centerpieces on dinner and refreshment tables, but these may be anything from a few sprigs to long garlands of blossoms. Just be sure that all arrangements on the bridal table are low so they won't obscure the members of the wedding party. You may even use your bridal bouquet in the center of the table, with those of your attendants lined up on either side of it. The cake table is usually decorated with floral sprays or other small arrangements. You may use floral screens and banks of ferns to form a background for the receiving line, but this is a matter of individual preference. The most effective floral decorations create a festive atmosphere without calling attention to themselves.

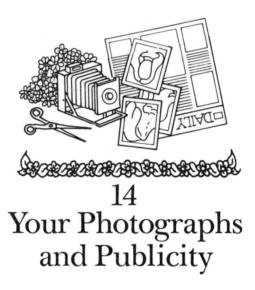

14
Your Photographs
and Publicity

YOUR MARRIAGE CEREMONY will be over in a few minutes, the reception in a few hours, but the photographs of your wedding will last a lifetime. Your bridal portrait, wedding candids and newspaper clippings are keepsakes you'll treasure for years to come. Through them, you and your groom will be able to relive some of your happiest moments and share your precious memories with others.

YOUR BRIDAL PORTRAIT

Your most important wedding photograph is your formal portrait, for it may be published in the newspapers and prominently displayed in your new home and those of your relatives. It's wise to keep both purposes in mind so you'll be proud of your portrait after it appears in the newspapers and sits on top of the piano for twenty years. Some backgrounds, lighting, hairstyles and makeup fail to pass the tests of time and newspaper reproduction.

Most newspapers require that wedding photographs be submitted one to two weeks before the scheduled publication date, so it may be necessary to have your portrait taken as much as a month before your wedding day. If the proper facilities are available, you may arrange to have it taken at the bridal salon during the final fitting of your dress. Otherwise, it's best to go to your photographer's studio where you can be sure of having the lighting, background, air conditioning and peaceful surroundings necessary for best results.

Your bridal portrait should look as if it was taken on your wedding day, so be sure you have all the proper accessories — shoes, petticoats, gloves, jewelry, prayer book — with you at the studio. Take along a detailed description of your bridal bouquet so the photographer can provide an appropriate dummy, if you want your portrait to show your flowers. Your hair and makeup should, of course, be at their best for your portrait sitting, but they should not be extreme. You should strive for a natural look, one that won't make your portrait look dated in a few years.

Before you make your final selection from the proofs, be sure to ask your photographer's advice about the poses that will look best in the newspapers. You may want to choose one pose for publicity purposes and a different one for your finished portrait. Most photographers supply the glossy prints required for newspaper publication at no additional charge.

YOUR WEDDING CANDIDS

The person who photographs your wedding ceremony and reception should be someone with the knowledge and experience to get the kind of pictures you'll display with pride. A talented friend or relative may be able to handle the job, but a professional photographer specializing in weddings is usually more reliable. This doesn't mean that your friends should be discouraged from bringing cameras to the wedding. Let them shoot all the pictures they want. As long as they don't have the complete responsibility, it won't matter if they get wrapped up in the wedding festivities and forget all about taking pictures.

Some of the wedding photographs classified as "candids" are not really candid at all, but the best ones usually are. The pictures that catch spontaneous action and unconscious facial expressions are those that mean the most as time goes by. It's nice to include a few posed photographs in your wedding album, but these should be kept to a minimum. Plan in advance to have them taken as quickly and unobtrusively as possible, for too much posing interferes with the wedding proceedings and festivities.

Whatever you do, don't make your guests wait around while you and the other members of the wedding party pose for pictures. If you want to be photographed with your parents or your bridesmaids, for example, you can allow time for these pictures to be taken at home as soon as you finish dressing. Since the bridal party leaves the church before any of the guests, you should arrive at the reception in time to pose for several pictures before the first guests appear. A formal shot of you and your groom and another of the entire wedding party might be taken at that time. The ushers and best man can be photographed after the receiving line forms, and any other posed pictures you want can be taken while you greet the guests.

Although a competent photographer doesn't need coaching to capture the highlights of a wedding, he does need to know your personal plans and wishes. You should make sure that he's familiar with any regulations, for some clergymen don't permit flash bulbs or altar photographs during the ceremony. And even if such pictures are permitted, you may not want them taken. After all, no picture is worth an intrusion upon the solemnity and dignity of your wedding ceremony.

PRE-WEDDING PUBLICITY

In large metropolitan areas, the only advance publicity a marriage receives is that published with the engagement announcement. (See Chapter I for suggested wording.) In many small communities, however, the activities surrounding an impending wedding make society-page news for weeks before the ceremony. Some papers report the details of showers and all other parties given in honor of the bride and groom, while others publish the wedding plans a week or two in advance. Such an item might read:

Plans for the marriage of Miss Cynthia Ann Bentley, daughter of Mr. and Mrs. Hugh Edward Bentley of Briarcliff Road, and Mr. James Sutton, son of Mrs. Richard Cole Sutton and the late Mr. Sutton of Chicago, Illinois, were announced today by the bride. The ceremony will be performed at the First Presbyterian Church of Lockport, with the Reverend Roger Saunders officiating.

Miss Bentley will be attended by her sister, Mrs. Michael McGovern of New York City as matron of honor. The bridesmaids will be Miss Phyllis Gunn of Shreveport, Louisiana, Miss Caroline Hoover, Miss Andrée Bronck and Mrs. Joseph Troy of Lockport. Miss Leslie McGovern, the bride's neice, will be flower girl. Dennis Russell of Chicago will be Mr. Sutton's best man. Michael McGovern, Stevenson Harris of Chicago, and Edward Fisher and Richard Hertz of Lockport will serve as ushers.

The ceremony will be followed by a reception at the White Hills Country Club.

Before submitting an item of this type, you should study your newspaper carefully to make sure it considers such information newsworthy, then follow the form usually used for such stories as closely as possible.

YOUR WEDDING ANNOUNCEMENT

It's customary to publish the pertinent details of a formal wedding in the couple's home town newspapers. A morning wedding is sometimes written up in an evening paper the same day, but most wedding stories are published the day after the ceremony. Check with your newspaper in advance to learn its exact requirements and deadlines. Some, for example, require the bride to fill out a standard form and submit it to the society editor a week before the wedding. Others want telephoned confirmation that the wedding has actually taken place before they will allow publication of the story.

If your paper does not supply wedding announcement forms, just type the information double-spaced on one side of plain white paper, $8\frac{1}{2} \times 11$ inches. Be sure to put your name, address and telephone number (or that of someone else in the community who can be called for verification and additional details) in the upper right-hand corner. The date you'd like the announcement published should appear in the upper left-hand corner.

If you want a photograph published with your wedding story, send an 8×10 glossy print of your bridal portrait along with the announcement details. A typed line of identification should be attached to the photo in case it gets separated from the story. Enclose the picture, announcement and a piece of stiff cardboard in a manila envelope and address it to the women's page editor. If you send photographs to more than one paper in the same city, you may want to submit different poses to each one.

A typical wedding announcement reads:

Miss Mary Clark Butler, daughter of Mr. and Mrs. Willard T. Butler of South Orange, was married this afternoon to Emile Claude Pomeroy, son of Mr. and Mrs. James C. Pomeroy of Short Hills. Msgr. Patrick Flynn of Englewood, uncle of the bride, performed the ceremony at Trinity Church in South Orange.

The bride, escorted by her father, wore an ivory dress of silk-faced peau de soie trimmed with Venise lace. Bands of matching lace trimmed her chapel train and fingertip veil. She carried a cascade of white roses and stephanotis.

Miss Carla Butler, sister of the bride, was the maid of honor. The bridesmaids were Misses Gloria Smith and Linda Kerr of South Orange, Mrs. Alexander McGinnis of Teaneck and Mrs. Kenneth Brophy of Buffalo, New York.

Thomas Buckley of Newark served as best man. The ushers were Richard Butler, brother of the bride, John Allison of Short Hills, and Edward Lyons and Francis Grayson of New York City.

Some newspapers also publish descriptions of the bridesmaids and mothers' dresses and flowers, the location of the reception, details of the newlyweds' respective educational backgrounds, professional affiliations, grandparents' names, honeymoon plans and other information. Use published stories in your paper as your guide to the type of detail to include.

Announcements of small weddings and second marriages usually don't go into detail, but include only the basic facts in the first paragraph, above. A prior marriage is sometimes mentioned in a line saying, "The bride's previous marriage ended in divorce."

If your parents are divorced, the announcement would read: ". . . the *daughter of Mrs. Clark Butler of South Orange and Mr. William T. Butler of New York City.*" If one of your parents is widowed, the correct phrasing is ". . . *the daughter of Mrs. William T. Butler and the late Mr. Butler.*" If your mother has remarried and you have been adopted by your stepfather, this information appears later in the story, perhaps in reporting that your stepfather gave you away.

15
Your Wedding Gifts

THE GIFTS YOU receive as a bride not only provide a nucleus for equipping and decorating your new home, but are wonderful tokens of friendship as well. Only those persons who accept invitations to your reception customarily send gifts, but you'll probably receive presents from others who are unable to attend. You may also receive packages from persons you don't even know, since it is customary for all gifts, even those from relatives of the groom, to be sent to the bride.

Your fiancé, your mother, your maid of honor and your bridesmaids may all want to join in the fun and help you open your gifts. Just be careful that no cards or essential details get lost in all the excitement. Keep accurate records to avoid mixing up gifts or omitting thank-you notes. If you haven't already received a wedding book that includes

147

a section for gifts, you should request or buy a gift-record book from your stationer, bridal salon or gift consultant.

As you open each package, list it immediately in your record book. Include an identifying description of the gift, the name and address of the donor, the store from which it came (in case you want to exchange it later), the date it arrived, and the date your thank-you note is mailed. If you expect a lot of gifts, it's best to attach a number corresponding to the listing on each one — then you'll know which silver candy dish came from your fiancé's great-aunt Susan. Most gift and wedding books include self-adhesive numbers for this purpose. You may want to enlist your maid of honor's help to keep your gift record.

YOUR THANK-YOU NOTES

Start writing your thank you notes as soon as you receive your first wedding presents. Putting them off just makes the task more difficult and causes hard feelings all around. You must write a personal, handwritten letter of appreciation for each gift you receive — even one from a close friend you've thanked in person and see every day. The only exceptions to this thanks-in-writing rule are gifts from your parents and from your fiancé.

Thank-you notes need not be long, but they should be prompt. In general you should try to acknowledge gifts that arrive more than a week before your wedding within two weeks of their arrival; those arriving later, within a month after your honeymoon. If you expect to receive more gifts than you could possibly acknowledge within this time, you might send engraved or printed cards to let your friends and relatives know their gifts arrived safely. These cards, which must be followed by personal notes as soon as possible, usually read:

Miss Catherine Barbara Russek
acknowledges with thanks
the receipt of your wedding gift
and will take pleasure in writing a personal note
at an early date.

Thank-you notes should be written in ink on a good grade of folded note paper. Your name or monogram may be engraved on the notes if you wish, but you won't use your married name or initial until after the wedding. Decorated notes and those with "Thank You" or "Mr. and Mrs." printed on them are inappropriate for thank-you notes, as are postcards with photographs or other gimmicks.

A thank-you letter to a married couple is usually addressed to the wife, but it's customary to mention her husband's name in the body of the note. It's also nice to mention your own husband or fiancé whenever possible. For example, you might begin, "*Dear Mrs. Clarke, Jimmy and I are delighted with the beautiful vase we received today from you and Mr. Clarke . . .*" Notes to relatives and close friends may be signed with your first name only, those to people you don't know well with both names. After the wedding, you may include your maiden name whenever necessary for identification. In other words, you might sign, "Susan Johnson" or "Susan Barnes Johnson," but never "Mrs. Steven Johnson." If you plan to continue using your maiden name socially as well as professionally after your wedding, you might choose this chance to signal your choice to your friends by signing your notes "Susan Barnes" even after the wedding.

It's much easier to make your thank-you notes sound sincere and spontaneous if you set aside time to write a few every day. If you try to write several dozen at once, it will be difficult to make them all sound truly appreciative. This is especially true if you postpone them until after your wedding.

When you write your thank-you notes, remember that each person receives only one, no matter how many you write. Each letter should sound as warm and as personal as you can make it. Avoid anything that might sound stuffy or gushy, but don't be afraid of exuberance. Almost everyone — especially older friends and family — loves enthusiastic praise of something chosen with care and affection. Refer to the individual gift and how you plan to use it whenever possible. If it's one of those inevitable mystery gifts with an obscure purpose, refer to it by color or material. It's much more gracious to say thanks for a specific ''blue glass piece'' or ''silver container'' than for a vague ''lovely gift.'' Try to put at least one thought besides thank you into each note. For example, you might include an invitation to visit, a comment about the wedding, a reference to your new apartment or some other personal touch.

Some thank-you notes are easier to write than others. Many brides find money gifts difficult to acknowledge, but these can be the easiest of all if you just mention how you plan to use the money. For example, the following would be appropriate to thank an uncle for a gift check.

Dear Uncle Cort,

Jim and I just this minute got in from furniture-scouting and found your very generous check in the mailbox. Thank you so much. This is the perfect answer to the question, Can we have that inlaid coffee table? Can't wait to have it, and you, in the new apartment.

We're both looking forward to seeing you at the wedding.
Affectionately,
Marjorie

Gifts that are part of a large set, such as place settings of china and silver usually have some special aspect that you can comment about. For example, you might write a good friend something like this:

Dear Jeannie,

Can't tell you how thrilled I was to get a complete place setting of our silver from you and your parents. You know how the elegant life suits us. This is our fifth place setting (Can you believe it?), and I can't wait to have the three of you for dinner, just as soon as we're settled.

We're looking forward to seeing you all at Sarah's next weekend.

Much love,
Cathy

For a gift from someone you don't know well — friends of your fiancé's parents, perhaps — write a more formal note. For example:

Dear Mrs. Holman,

Thank you so much for the silver drink muddlers. They're very handsome; we've never seen anything quite like them.

Jim talks so often about you and Doctor Holman and the Sundays he spent at your house when he was growing up that I can't wait to meet you both.

Again, thanks for thinking of us.

Best,
Susanna Barnes

Unique gifts — a rare antique or something handmade —

merit special attention. Even if you don't like them, you should praise the originality or workmanship.

If a gift arrives late, you should either ignore the fact or make it a point of special pleasure. For example, the following note might be sent to a friend of your in-laws:

Dear Miss Baker,

What a nice surprise to find your gift when I arrived home from work yesterday! It turned a routine day into something almost like Christmas. The one thing our apartment needed most was a table lamp, and you've found the perfect one! Do I detect collusion with Steve's mother? Steve and I are both delighted.

Most sincerely,
Susanna Johnson

If you receive a single gift from a large group — your fiancé's co-workers or fellow members of an organization, perhaps — one thank-you note addressed to the group is sufficient. If the joint gift is from several relatives, bridesmaids or friends, however, you should write each one a separate letter. Make each note a personal expression of your appreciation, not just a carbon copy of the others.

PRESENTS ON DISPLAY

The custom of displaying wedding gifts should not be considered ostentatious, for nearly everyone enjoys admiring a bride's presents — especially when his own holds a place of honor. Some guests even wait until they've examined the gift display before they select a wedding present.

Wedding presents are usually displayed in some part of the house that is not in constant use. Rows of card tables covered with fine white tablecloths or snowy sheets may be used to hold the gifts. You will probably start your display as soon as you have six or eight gifts, rearranging them as more come in. Group gifts into categories, with silver on one table, glassware on another, electrical appliances on a third. Display only token place settings of china, flat silver and crystal. Scatter similar gifts so that it's not obvious to anyone that you received twelve sets of salt and pepper shakers. If you file the gift cards elsewhere, you can display just one set of exact duplicates and each donor will think you've received only his own. Modest gifts should not be made to suffer comparison next to extravagant gifts. Do not display money gifts. Garlands of greens, small bowls of flowers or clusters of ribbon from the packages may make your display more festive.

It's always wise to take out a temporary floater policy insuring your gifts while they are on display. If you receive many valuable presents, you may also want to hire a detective to guard them during the ceremony and other times when the house will be empty.

If your reception is held in your home, your guests will see the gifts at that time. Receptions in other locations do not include a gift display. You may ask friends to come over informally to see the gifts or give a special luncheon, tea or bridesmaids' party to show them. Gift displays are often left intact for a week after the ceremony so friends and relatives can drop by to see them.

DAMAGED GIFTS

Gifts that arrived damaged must be handled with great tact. If you receive one from a local store, return it for replacement. If it comes from an out-of-town store, write a letter of explanation and wait for their instructions. Be sure to ask them not to mention the breakage to the donor. More than one bride has neglected to make such a request, only to learn that the store did call the donor after she'd sent a thank-you note with no mention of the damage. If a broken gift was mailed by the giver, check the wrappings to see if it was insured. If so, you may return it with a note of explanation so the donor can collect the insurance and make the replacement. You should never mention damage to an uninsured or nonreturnable gift, however, as it may make the donor feel obliged to send another. Damaged gifts are never displayed unless they can be arranged so the damage is not obvious.

EXCHANGES

No matter how careful you are about registering your gift preferences, you'll probably receive at least a few presents you can't use. Some duplicates — especially of breakable items — are nice to have, but no bride really needs more than one silver candle snuffer. It's both proper and practical to exchange duplicates, but no one likes to think his gift was one of the ones returned. If you receive exact duplicates or other items than can be exchanged without the giver's knowing, go ahead. Otherwise, it's only right to keep the gift so your Aunt Agatha won't be hurt to discover that the silver candlesticks she so carefully selected never found a place in your new home. Never ask where a gift was purchased so you can exchange it, and don't mention duplication or exchange in your thank-you notes. Those persons who are not offended by exchanges seldom make them necessary.

RETURNS

When a wedding is merely postponed, you send an announcement to all the guests (see Chapter V), and keep the presents you've already received. When a wedding is cancelled, however, every gift — even those that have been monogrammed — must go back to the person who sent it. A note expressing gratitude and explaining that the wedding will not take place accompanies each present, but you need give no reason for the cancellation.

MONOGRAMMING

There was a time when almost every wedding gift — silver, glassware or linens — bore a monogram. Today, however, most brides prefer to have any monogramming done after the wedding. This way you can avoid the "no exchange" rule that usually applies to monogrammed gifts, and make sure your monograms will be uniform. Even if your friends don't follow the old custom of putting the bride's maiden initials on gifts purchased before the wedding, there's a good chance that monograms created by different persons at different times just won't match.

A monogram is a personal trademark that should be chosen with care. The most common one for silver is a single initial, usually your married surname, engraved on the handles. Triple-initial monograms are also popular, especially for linens. These may follow any one of a variety of styles, including triangles, circular scrolls and simple rectangles. The bride's first, maiden and married initials are the usual choice, but you may also use your first initial, your husband's first initial and your common initial above or below the other two. If your initials spell a word, like *BAD* or *JAR*, choose a monogram design in which the last initial is in the center and larger than the other two: *bDa* or *jRa*.

GIFTS FOR ATTENDANTS

You and your groom will probably follow tradition and give each of your attendants a small gift as a token of appreciation and as a memento of the occasion. These need not be expensive, but are usually relatively permanent items of a personal nature. You should give identical gifts to each bridesmaid, but your maid of honor's present should be a little more special. The same holds true for the gifts your fiancé gives his ushers and best man. Attendants' gifts are always distributed before the wedding — often at the bridesmaids' luncheon and bachelor party or at the rehearsal dinner.

You may give your attendants almost anything you think they'll like, but the customary gift is one that can be worn in the wedding or monogrammed and engraved with the wedding date. In the first category are gifts of gloves, pearls or earrings for the bridesmaids (or their bridesmaids' dresses, if you wish to relieve them of this expense); studs, cufflinks, tie bars or stickpins for the ushers. Girls' gifts suitable for engraving include silver compacts, bracelets, gold pins and cigarette lighters or cases. For men, money clips, belt buckles, key holders, stud boxes and pen and pencil sets are often chosen. Or you may break with tradition and give each attendant a book or record chosen for each one's interests.

GIFTS TO EACH OTHER

There is no rule of etiquette that says you and your groom must exchange gifts, but most couples do. They choose gifts they know will be treasured for years, for their usefulness as well as for their sentimental value. For example, you might give your groom a fine watch, a pair of gold cuff links, a piece of luggage, an attaché case or a handsome wallet. He, on the other hand, might give you a watch, a string of cultured pearls, fine luggage, a silver dresser set or heirloom jewelry.

GIFT REMINDER LIST

List all your presents in a record book the moment they are opened.

Write down a description of the gift, the name of the giver, the store and the date received. Leave a space to write the date when your thank-you note is mailed. Paste a number on each gift corresponding to that in the book.

Set up tables and have them covered for displaying your gifts. (Long cloths can provide a hiding place for boxes you'll want to repack for shipment to your new home.)

Arrange the gifts as they arrive to protect them from harm.

Rearrange your gifts, whenever necessary.

Make sure your presents are safe — insured, if possible.

Acknowledge the receipt of each gift with a personal note as soon as possible.

Check over your records frequently so you can thank the donors in person whenever you see them.

16
Wedding Guests

ALTHOUGH A WEDDING guest's chief function is to share the happiness of the bride and groom and wish them well, certain customs and conventions should be observed.

RECEIVING A WEDDING INVITATION

A formal invitation to a wedding ceremony doesn't require a response unless a pew card is enclosed, but an invitation to a reception must be acknowledged promptly. A guest should always write a formal note of acceptance or regret, whether the invitation requests a reply or not. A verbal acceptance is not enough, no matter how close the relationship with the bride. When "the pleasure of your company" is requested, a formal response is expected.

A reply to a formal invitation is written on a double sheet of fine notepaper, not on an informal, a printed card or decorated paper. It is written in the third person, with the wording and spacing similar to that on the engraved invitation. It is not necessary to repeat the name of the bride and groom, but repeating the time and date shows that these have been understood correctly. The inclusion of the place is optional, but can explain the absence of a guest who lives in New York, for example, and is declining an invitation to a wedding in St. Louis.

The typical formal acceptance reads:

Mr. and Mrs. David Mott Orr
accept with pleasure
the invitation of
Mr. and Mrs. John Carr Blake
for Saturday the fourth of April
at half after four o'clock

A formal regret is usually worded:

Mr. and Mrs. David Mott Orr
regret that they are unable to accept
the kind invitation of
Mr. and Mrs. John Carr Blake
for Saturday, the fourth of April

A personal note is the correct response to an informal, handwritten invitation to a wedding or reception. For example:

Dear Andrea,

Jack and I are delighted to be included among the guests at Josie's wedding on the fourth of April at Holy Trinity Chapel. We are looking forward to both the ceremony and the reception.

Affectionately,
Becky

An informal note of regret might read:

Dear Alicia,

Peter and I regret that we will be away on the fifth of June, as my younger sister is graduating that day. If we hadn't already made plans, you know nothing could keep us from Becky's wedding.

Please send Becky and Jim our best wishes for their future happiness.

Fondly,
Susan

RECEIVING A WEDDING ANNOUNCEMENT

A wedding announcement does not obligate the recipient in any way; neither a gift nor an acknowledgement is necessary. When dear friends are involved, however, it's courteous to send a personal note of good wishes to the couple, and perhaps to their parents as well.

SENDING A WEDDING GIFT

An invitation to a wedding ceremony alone does not require a gift, and neither does a reception invitation that is declined. Those who are close enough to the couple to be invited to the reception often do send gifts even if they're unable to attend and always if they do.

A wedding gift should be sent to the bride at her home as soon as possible after the invitation is received. It may be mailed or sent directly from the store. It's customary to enclose one's personal card — with a wish for the couple's happiness written across the top — with the gift. Married couples always use "Mr. and Mrs." cards even when only one of them knows the bride and groom.

Gifts sent after the wedding are addressed to both bride and groom at their new address. If illness or absence is responsible for the delay, it's customary to enclose a note explaining why the present is late.

A wedding gift should be chosen with careful thought and an eye to practicality. It need not be expensive or in keeping with the size or style of the wedding. Sometimes it's a very modest gift chosen with imagination and affection that pleases the couple most of all. If a guest is unfamiliar with the couple's tastes, it's best to play safe and give them china, silver or some other item listed with their gift registry. Attempts to be cute or original often turn out to be white elephants. Money also makes a suitable, and always appreciated, wedding gift. Checks sent before the wedding are made out to the bride; those given on the wedding day or later are made out to Mr. and Mrs.

DRESSING FOR A WEDDING

Wedding guests dress as they would for almost any other social event at the same hour and season. Men usually wear suits and women wear street-length costumes in any color except all white or all black. Modest necklines, gloves and hats or other head coverings are in order for women in most churches, but the hats may be removed for the reception. Guests may wear formal attire to large formal weddings in the evening.

CHURCH WEDDING PROCEDURES

Guests without reserved pew cards should arrive at the site of the ceremony about thirty minutes before the appointed time, or earlier for a very large gathering. Guests with reserved seats should arrive about twenty minutes before the ceremony. No guest should arrive later than ten minutes before the time set for the ceremony to begin. Guests arriving later should seat themselves quietly or remain in the rear of the church during the ceremony.

When they arrive at the church, guests are met in the vestibule by an usher who asks whether they are friends of the bride or groom. The right side of the aisle facing the altar is for the groom's relatives and friends, the left side for the bride's in Christian weddings. (These directions are reversed for Orthodox and Conservative Jewish ceremonies.) A friend of both the bride and groom says so and is seated in the best available seat. A woman guest takes the usher's right arm and is escorted down the aisle to her seat. Her husband or male escort walks a few steps behind them. It is customary for guests and ushers to carry on polite conversation in low tones as they walk down the aisle. Quiet conversation with other guests is also proper until the wedding processional begins.

It is not necessary for guests to carry out unfamiliar rituals, especially if their own faith forbids, but it's polite to follow the lead of the families seated in the front pews. Generally guests of another faith are expected to stand when the families stand, but may remain seated rather than kneeling.

After the recessional, guests remain in their seats until the ushers have escorted the families of the bride and groom, including the grandmothers and other close relatives sitting in the family pews.

AT THE RECEPTION

All reception guests pass along the receiving line, greeting and shaking hands with everyone. A guest who doesn't know the bride's mother introduces himself so she can pass his name on down the line. It's customary to make some remark about the wedding, the bride or the newly married couple, depending on how well one knows the persons involved. It's proper to congratulate the groom, but the bride is traditionally wished happiness. Considerate guests always move quickly down the line so that others are not kept waiting behind them. Women usually wear their gloves in the receiving line.

Once past the receiving line, guests go directly to the area where refreshments are being served. If it's a seated luncheon or dinner, they should seek their reserved places, or choose a seat at one of the unreserved tables. At a tea or cocktail reception, they may serve themselves and circulate. It's customary for wedding guests to introduce themselves to one another whenever necessary. If it's a reception at home, guests are often invited to see the wedding gifts before they leave. After all the guests have been received, the second stage of the reception begins. The wedding party take their places at the bridal table and the traditional toasts are proposed. Every guest should drink to every toast — if only with ginger ale. After the toasts, the meal is served or the bride and groom cut the wedding cake. At a stand-up reception, the bride and groom may begin the dancing before they cut the cake.

Wedding receptions have no specified length, but the festivities usually continue as long as the bride and groom remain. Once they have made their going-away dash through a shower of rice or rose petals, however, guests are usually expected to take their leave. The customary farewell to the host and hostess is not always possible at a wedding party, but a few words of praise for the occasion are sure to be appreciated.

17
Going Away

As THE HONORED guests, you and your groom may stay and enjoy your reception as long as you like, but it's customary to leave while the festivities are still in full swing. When you're ready to make your departure, just pass the word to your bridesmaids and other single friends to prepare to catch your bouquet. A stairway leading to the room where you plan to change is the most appropriate place from which to throw your flowers.

Your maid of honor goes with you to help you change, and the best man accompanies the groom. If you are traveling, be sure your going-away outfit is comfortable to sit in and will arrive at your first night's destination unrumpled. Your groom will probably wear a suit for going away.

When you are both dressed, packed and ready to go, word should be sent to your parents so they can come to say goodbye in private. This is apt to be a difficult moment for them, so try to be as thoughtful and understanding as you can. Let them know how much you appreciate everything they've done. When your groom has finished telling his own parents goodbye, he will come for you and thank your parents. After that, you both return to the reception to bid your guests farewell.

You may be tempted to leave the reception quietly through a back door, but your guests will never forgive you if you try to sneak away. Supplies of rice will be distributed to the guests while you are changing. Flower petals — either real or paper — are sometimes substituted for rice, but traditionalists stick with the ancient symbol of fertility and plenty. A shower of rice may not be the easiest thing to run through, but it's a lot easier to get out of your clothes than confetti.

Once you've been showered by your friends on your mad dash to the getaway car, you're on your way. The best man will have taken care of putting the luggage in the car and keeping practical jokers away. When you reach your destination, it's nice to send a telegram or flowers to each of your homes to let your parents know you arrived safely and to thank them for the wedding.

When you begin summing up your memories, you'll both realize that your own wedding has a special beauty and meaning for you no other ceremony will ever match. Whether it's a simple family service or an elaborate ritual, your wedding will always have a special place in your heart. It is, after all, the beginning of your life together. May it be a long, prosperous and increasingly happy one.

Index

171